OPEN MIKE

(Poetry for Plebs)

By Michael J Davidson

For those who prefer Poetry to be easy to read and even easier to understand

Published by New Generation Publishing in 2015

Copyright © Michael J Davidson 2015

First Edition

www.newgeneration-publishing.com

 New Generation Publishing

Whatever you can do

Or think you can

Begin it.

Boldness has genius

Power,

And magic in it.

Goethe

Foreword

Mike Davidson is a prolific writer who never lets quantity lessen the quality of his poetry. Like all the best writers, he writes about what he knows and what we all can relate to. He has a knack of saying, 'I'm like this, are you?' and invariably we nod in reply.

He is an extremely popular member of the Jewish Poetry Society. His humorous poems always make us laugh (or groan!) and his political poems have been known to bring cheers of agreement. Mike is an expert at putting his words to music and, being a talented musician, often accompanies himself on accordion or keyboard.
We hope he remains a member of the JPS for many years to come.

Judy Karbritz (Harrow Community Poet and co-founder of the JPS with Pattie Greenberg)

www.jewishpoetrysociety.com

Writing poetry is often joyous, sometimes painful and sometimes revealing. "Open Mike" reflects this creative journey. Written in his inimitable style, Mike's poetry is woven with emotion from anger through to smiles. This expressive and personal collection has something for every mood, laugh-out-loud to crying softly.

Avril Candler

'I am a huge fan of Mike's poetry. He has the ability to entertain, educate, uplift and frequently move to laughter and tears ... sometimes all within one poem! A truly gifted writer of truly enjoyable verse.'

SIOBHAN CURHAM Award winning Author, Editor and Speaker.

INDEX

THOUGHTS IN AN MRI SCANNER 7

WHY 8

WHEN WILL WE/THEY EVER LEARN? 9

A FATHER'S LAMENT 10

A GRANDFATHER'S LAMENT 11

MEMORIES 12

MY PILLOW FULL OF DREAMS 13

ANOTHER YEAR............... 14

CHOICES 15

BELOW THE RADAR 16

FREEDOM PASS 17

ABSENT FRIENDS............. 18

PERHAPS 19

GHOSTS AT THE TABLE....20

MY SECRET DESIRE 21

PAPERWORK 22

NO BOUNDARIES 23

POPPIES 23

PASSING PARADE............ 24

PSYCHIC 26

QUADRANGULATION...... 27

RANDOM RHYME... RANDOM REASON 28

RECIPES FOR DREAMS 29

REEVA............................... 30

A WHITER SHADE OF PALE 31

REFLECTIONS 32

REPRISE ON REFLECTIONS 33

ROMANTIC CONCEIT OF FREEDOM 34

RUMMAGE 35

SACRIFICE........................ 36

SECRETS OR KEEPING SHTUM 37

SHADOWS, ... 38

SO WHAT'S NEW? 39

SORROW..........................40

STIRRING STUFF 41

THAT TIME OF YEAR........ 42

THE 6 A.M. POEM 43

THE AMOROUS PLUMBER
.... 44

THE BELT OF LIFE 45

THE BOTTOM OF THE HILL
(1).................................... 46

THE BOTTOM OF THE HILL
(2) 46

THE COMMON TOUCH ... 47

THE KNOCKOUT 48

THE WAY WE LIVE AND DIE
.... 49

THE WIDOW.................... 50

TIME OF YEAR 51

TOGETHERNESS 52

UNDECIDED 53

VOICES 54

WHAT IF?????? 55

CRUMBS 56

A JEWESS OF TODAY 57

GENERATION GAME 57

LOVE 58

LOSS 58

MUSIC 58

A PHONE CALL 59

A VIEW FROM MY ROOM 60

A ROW OF BOTTLES 61

BITTERNESS 62

SILENCE 62

WILDERNESS 62

DESERT 63

DESOLATION 63

CROWS KNOW 63

A TIME OF LONGING 64

A MONOLOGUE WITH
HASHEM 65

AFTER THE RAIN............. 66

"DRINK, MY DARLING?"...67

AN ENCOUNTER 68

CROATIA 70

BARBARIANS AT THE GATE
.... 71

BENDING THE RULES 72

BINMANIA 74

BLOOM 75

BURIED TREASURE........... 77

BY THE SEA 78

CHILDHOOD.................... 80

CONTAINED IN SPACE AND
TIME ?? 81

DOMESTIC DENTAL DRAMA 82

THE GIRL WITH THE MOBILE PHONE 83

THE GIFT 84

FUTURE PROOFING 85

LOOKING DOWN 85

PRACTICE GETS RESULTS 86

PRACTICE MAKES PERFECT 87

THE FIVE SENSES 89

WHISPERS 90

A WRITER'S PROSETTE 91

PAPERWORK 2 92

ALIEN BLOOD 93

ODOUR OF HAMAS 93

MY BEST ASSET 94

SINGULAR STATISTIC 95

CHALLENGE 96

DAY BY DAY BY DAY 97

DISCOVERY 98

THE LIFT 99

THE LIST 100

MY GREATEST FEAR 101

MIXING THE SENSES 102

GIDDY MOMENT 103

EPITAPH TO JIM 104

FASHION 105

THE PAIN OF SEPARATION 107

INTO THE VOID 108

THE ROOM OF NOT KNOWING 109

HARROW ON THE HILL .. 110

PATHWAY 111

MIRROR MIRROR 112

OPENING 113

JUNK 114

I WISH 115

ODE TO OSAMA 116

MY BEST FRIEND 117

OFF AND ON 118

IT'S NOT ENOUGH 119

HOW TO COMPLAIN 120

THE JURY 121

LITTLE BOY 122

STAIN 123

THE HIPPOCRATIC OATH 124

THE ART OF LOSING 125

SUNMANIA 126

THE CATCH 127

STILL COMPETITIVE 128

THE ATTIC 129

LET THERE BE LIGHT...... 130

ON BEING A FATHER OF
THE BRIDE-TO-BE............131

FRATERNITY 132

O DAUGHTER MY
DAUGHTER...................... 133

I'M ALONE 134

STIFF UPPER LIP 135

SEMITIC SIAMESE 136

MILK AND HONEY 137

IN RECLINE...................... 138

FOG 139

TXT RYM 140

THE CHAIR BENEATH THE
TREE.................................141

FOOTWEAR FAILURE 142

MALIGNANCY.................. 143

UNREQUITED 144

VAITING AND VAITING .. 145

PAVLOVA PANIC 147

WIND 149

FRANCIS ALBERT : 15TH
MAY, 1998......................... 150

EMPTYNESS..................... 151

DEATH 151

THOUGHTS IN AN MRI SCANNER

I'm in a tube that clicks,

repeatedly.

I cannot and must not move.

That's obligatory.

My body lies defenceless,

horizontally.

I tell myself the time will pass,

hypnotically.

My tissues are being dissected,

magnetically.

They watch me through Perspex,

unconcernedly.

I will be told what's wrong.

Eventually.

25.02 1996

WHY

Why, Grandad is your beard so grey?
And why Grandad, do you walk that way?
With a funny little limp like you're leaning right over,
and can't keep up with pet dog Rover!
Why, Grandma, do you cry and cry?
What makes you so sad when we say goodbye?
Why do you live so far, far away?
Why can't you come to our house and stay?
Why can't you hear me when I'm on the phone?
Why are the two of you so all alone?
I wonder, when we kiss and hug each other,
don't you also have a father and a mother?
Why don't you tell me to just keep quiet and why are you
always going on diet?
It isn't because you're much too fat, you don't wanna die,
I'm sure it's that.
But we all have to die, you told me so,
'cept we have much longer than you to go.
So Gran and Gramps don't die too soon,
can't you wait till late this afternoon?
We love you too much to lose you just now...
with many more years may God you both endow!

28.2.2013

WHEN WILL WE/THEY EVER LEARN?

I tried to be liberal, I really did try,
I do try my utmost, to adore Stephen Fry!
But when I see headlines like those of the day
my most basic instincts scream, some other way!
Our troops being killed by Afghans they train,
squandering resources, all wasted in vain.
We let Moat out of prison, to kill and to maim
then make out he's a hero, for his victims, what a shame!
Let criminals go free! That's the mantra we hear...
while innocent folks stay indoors full of fear.
We pay Europe's greedy, with huge sums of our gold...
then welcome their multitudes, for OUR benefit we are told!!!
Our politician's promises before they were elected,
within a few months, all or most are rejected!
We are taxed to the hilt, it's for our own good,
then see our MP's claim far more than they should.
Our wild feral youths roam the streets causing havoc,
waving ASBO'S aloft while they all run amok.
Surely now is the time to bring back sterner measures...
few strokes on the bottom with canes or with leather!!!
No more TV's in jail, let them slop like before....
no more halving of sentences make them longer, much more.
Stop the flood through our borders, make them far more secure,
reduce welfare benefits, honest work is the cure.
But apart from all this, let us stop the pretence
that Britain's still a World Power, it doesn't make sense,
to go on bombing people all over the place,
to help our US Allies losing much too much face!
So who should we vote for, I'll give you one guess
Enoch Powell, where are you? Come clean up this mess!

14.07.2010

A FATHER'S LAMENT

I'm missing you, my little shadow,

more than words can say,

beyond my deepest imaginings,

with every passing day.

Recalling all those halcyon years before your independence,

prior to cosmic convictions gaining exclusive ascendance.

Irreplaceable life's ingredient

for us has now gone missing...

since happy childhood days and years

with all the hugs and kissing...

you have vanished like a whirlwind

maybe gone from us forever...

will we ever meet again?

A voice inside me whispers 'Never!'

25.10. 2012

A GRANDFATHER'S LAMENT

Echoes of children's laughter, salt tears from injured knees...
longest words from little lips, "can we stay up later please?"
Early morning waking-up, endless tidying chores...
why is Grandpa still asleep?
And wow! How loud he snores!
Grandpa, put your seat belt on!
You know you're being naughty!
Can see you're driving much too fast...
the clock says more than forty!
But how you miss their presence when
grandkids are not around...
the empty house so silent, discarded toys don't sound.
All year you spent in longing, for few short weeks together...
and when they're with you time flies fast
you pray for sunny weather!
Then it's over, much too soon,
what more could you have done?
To make their stay outstanding
overflowing with joy and fun?

The taxi's waiting, bags are packed...
all eyes display a tear...
They come and give you those huge hugs...
"We'll see you soon .....next year!"

21.08. 2013

MEMORIES

Seemingly inconsequential things

triggering floods of fond remembrance.

A phrase, few notes of a song,

a face, swiftly disappearing in a crowd.

That familiar fragrance lost on the breeze...

then frustratingly, clarity fades.

Details disperse.

You are left clutching desperately at jumbled recollections,

hoping slivers will expand,

might suddenly resurface...and sometimes they do

but when you least expect!

Keep albums up to date, films revamped on DVD,

above all, do not forget..keep taking the tablets,

they do work, you know!

12.06.2013

MY PILLOW FULL OF DREAMS

Moments minuscule pass by, as soft cheek touches down

on cool-at-first pale cover, just before they all arrive.

Princes, flaxen locks adrift, glistening blades aloft,

Barbie-doll maidens, tiny-waisted, alluring en route to the Ball.

Venomous villains with sharp yellow teeth,

savage-eyed beasties dripping drool as they charge.

Sudden scene changes...wavelets splash on the sand,

feet sink in the shallows...ain't the seaside just grand!

Now clouds threaten darkly, dead-black night swallows all.

Whirling, falling, grabbing, missing, eyes open or can it be real?

Will earth-fall be a source of pain?

Hands reach out but seize on nothing, where have Prince and Princess gone?

Is the passage leading somewhere or a mere blank wall to greet me?

Will my mum and dad be there or someone bad to meet me?

Now my pillow feels on fire, I think I need to run...

oh, how I wish the dawn would come, I need to see the sun!

Just a nightmare, 'twill be said, but I think I'll jump in Grandma's bed!

Dedicated to Maya, my beloved grand-daughter, who coined the title!
(01.09.2010)

ANOTHER YEAR

Another year, another birthday,

silver out-flanks the black...

fatal time for looking forward,

worse for looking back.

Philosophise but at your peril...

what was it all about?

What's been left behind you as you start your slow way out?

It's like an old-time movie show, the cartoons, then the news...

the main big picture nears THE END

no wonder one gets the blues.

Those who love you will remember for a while it's true...

then as years roll grimly by they will forget you too.

Except on days when they look back and sadly heave a sigh...

"What fun we had with grandpa"

then quietly they'll cry...

10.05.2012

CHOICES

Nothing could ever have prepared me.

My mere three decades of life,

imbued with hope, ambition, enthusiasm.

A measure of happiness, that was yesterday.

This is today. Now. Nine twenty five.

A clear blue, sunlit day.

I have choices.

Below me the fires of hell.

Above me desperation.

Screams.

Behind me my open plan nine to five previous existence.

Before me clean fresh air,

polluted by kerosene.

As I fly will my years kaleidoscope before me,

or will ninety-five floors take long?

Written after being turned off a flight at 9.00 am Philadelphia Airport on 11th September 2001 and spending six days in Philadelphia watching repeated showing of the World Trade Centre attacks. We had been visiting the WTC only one week previously.

BELOW THE RADAR

Glistening smile, deepest liquid pool eyes,

glow of health and happiness all stare out at me

from a portrait, painted not so long ago.

Now my view through the trees no longer lulls me to dreamless sleep.

No longer fills me with contentment I once knew.

For the face is now mere image,

my mind's memory of one so beloved

yet so distant as to be no longer.

Words 'below the radar' resonate, acutely causing pain

of separation, of longing, of nightmarish imaginings.

Where can you be? What possible cause?

In our minds we search, find no answers.

Silence like a cancer grows

then slays with infinite distance.

'So far below the radar' telephonic tones relay...

Is this our just dessert?

23.11 2011

FREEDOM PASS

This little plastic packet, an indigo shade of blue,

enables me to go wherever, on bus or train or tube.

Inside's a flattering picture, of me looking my best,

a pity it's only head and neck, 'cos I'm sticking out my chest!

Each time I place it where I must, I look around all flustered,

I know guards think I'm under age, for I retain my youthful lustre!

In fact I feel quite guilty at having these free rides,

but still I travel the tube all day and a few bus trips besides!

Who am I to question this largesse to one and all?

I paid my taxes all my life now on Transport I'm having a ball!

It's really meant for an ageing gent and wife to travel for free...

instead of which it gives the rich a bonus quite unnecessary!

One of these days I know for sure they'll means test the likes of me...

I'll have to depend on the chauffeur and Rolls

to claim Social Security!

05.03.2015

ABSENT FRIENDS

Fading sepia print, corners curling, faces frozen,

wreathed in structured smiles.

So long ago, straining to reminisce, what we all did,

what we all thought, planned, looked forward to.

So many gone before their time, lives lived, celebrated or regretted.

Misty-eyed I see their images and wonder...

could they, could we, in our innocence then,

have had an inkling, merest minimal foreknowledge

of what we'd become, achieve, succeed or fail?

Now, with full awareness, I see so clear,

like in some pictorial sequence, blanks where friends once were,

in graveyards far removed, or urns on dusty mantels.

Thankful, to whom I'm not quite sure,

I raise my glass and sip

to memories of absent friends.

13.05.2012

PERHAPS

Perhaps there never was a beginning, Big Bang so hard to believe...

perhaps there never will be an ending,

theory equally hard to conceive.

Perhaps if we accept that infinity

means no boundaries of time nor of space...

then the faith-led belief in divinity

can be shelved by the whole human race!

Beware when scientists all clamour 'our "Universe" was once so much smaller.'

'From where did it grow?' I just stammer,

'when it's huge will we all then stand taller?'

Perhaps after conflicts our earth has known,

as Humanity fights and splits...

by the time our "Universe" is 'fully grown'

perhaps we'll have blown us to bits!

28.05.2014

GHOSTS AT THE TABLE

I close my eyes.

I feel their presence.

I turn and stare...

they do not disappear.

Indentations on cushioned seats

where they once all sat still remain.

I see them everywhere,

on crowded pavements,

jostling in impatient queues.

But most of all when I come back home

and dine at my father's table.

Alone, in their spirited company,

I know they are there.

22.04.2015

MY SECRET DESIRE

Essential aspect 'bout this subject matter

is that it's personal, don't you agree?

So that if I divulge innermost urges to this widely acclaimed company,

I can no longer see in my bathroom

mirror image of private unexpurgated me!

Imagine if you will the ghastly sequelae

of blurting out my drives and preferences.

Once you've departed these palatial premises,

the whole of North London will have my bodily references!

There'll be twittering and texting around Brent Cross,

Golders Green will be up in arms!

How come we all were not forewarned

to prevent young ladies succumbing to his charms?

So No! Dearest ladies and sentimental gents,

on this occasion I must firmly refuse to expose my valued internal passions

for the lip-smacking enjoyment of Stanmore's Jews!!!

So There!

07.01. 2015

PAPERWORK

(Gotta pick a pocket or two...Lionel Bart's Oliver)

*When a cop makes an arrest... dirty old man touches young girl's
breast...
locks him up in jail all night but... he's got to do the paperwork too,
Sarge,
Gotta do the paper work too!
Go to the doctors when you feel ill ...he'll just prescribe another
pill...
makes you wait for hours and hours cos... he's gotta do the
paperwork too...
shame ...he's gotta do the paperwork too!
When you want to rent a car... you're in a rush, going far.
Half your holiday's gone because ...they have to do the Paperwork
too oy!
They have to do the Paperwork too!
I'm too lax when paying tax... couldn't I just send a fax?
Inland Revenue drives me nuts ....and so does all the paperwork too
hey!
And so does all the paperwork too!
When you marry Chupah is nice... Rabbi's giving you wise advice...
it's nearly time to fress and dance but... he's gotta do the paperwork
too....NU!
He's gotta do the Ketubah too!
When you die it doesn't stop ...for inheritance tax your cash they'll
crop...
funeral costs are high but nu?... your kids'll do the paperwork too,
so....
your kids'll do the paperwork too!
One last thing I ask of you ...I know that we all must use the loo...
but for royal arseholes in those big castles
who's doing all the paperwork there hey?
This is just not very nice and that is why I'm asking twice!
For royal arseholes in those big castles..... who is doing the
paperwork there??????*

22.01.2015

NO BOUNDARIES

Close your eyes,
liquidity of darkness,
fleeting willow-wisp images
floating, beyond grasping,
patterns changing
in shadowy light,
boundless dreamy vistas
of restless imagining.
Close your eyes...
surely you can see infinity
but can you see truth?

POPPIES

Blood-red tide rises up the ancient wall,
contemplating lives lost in battles fought in mud.
That was then.
Now sand-blown troops return from lands
awash with gore,
where poppies proliferate
sustaining life for those whose existence survives
on destroying mind and young bodies
with the evil pestilence
poppies provide.

23.10. 2013

PASSING PARADE

Reclining on an inflatable sun-lounger.
Soles of my feet seared by baking sea sand.
Eyelids droop. Drifting.
Shadow obstructs the sun.
My eyes open.

Smiling ebony face, glittering enamel-white grin.
"HELLO!!! Watches, Rolex, Omega ,Tag Heuer, New Film
DVD's!!!
Cheap...just eight euros!!!"
I shake my head, he departs. Slowly. Reluctantly.
Sun's rays warm pale flesh once more.
Eyes shut.

"Massage, very good, very deep!"
Oriental smile, diminutive figurine.
Thankfully not obscuring my sun!
Paper-thin, she carries a collapsible stretcher.
I check my musculature, decline her ministrations.
Smile fades, almond eyes glazed, disappointed.

Blessed unconsciousness once again envelops me.
Skin colour darkening imperceptibly, I am certain.

"Fresh Pineapple, ice cream, drinks, Sangria!"
This time swarthy Mediterranean countenance, sweating
visibly.
I turn over disdainfully.
Time to do my back, I think!

"Senor, you must pay for your sunbed, por favor!"
Things definitely looking up.
Twisting and turning I do look up.
Voluptuous blonde nymphet,
complete with money-pouch and credit card machine.
Economically-clad bikini partly hiding nothing at all.
Frantic search for elusive wallet. Pay cash.
She flounces merrily on her way.

.

Reflecting chance missed I surrender....
to fully-paid-up uninterrupted sun-roasted sleep.
Suddenly..... cold wet sensation.
High tide! Freak wave! I am immersed.
Time to dry off, pack up and go home!

23.09. 2013 (guess where)

PSYCHIC

She seemed to know my every move

my life to her was one long groove...

predictable she called me, grinning, aware when I was losing or winning.

Could she be called a sensitive, or perhaps a touch intuitive?

Whether I was here or there she'd know for sure exactly where!

And if I spoke the truth or lied it'd be no use, with her wide-eyed,

she'd laugh and taunt, and know for sure my very next move, chaste or impure!

How did she do it, was she gifted,

with second sight which never shifted?

It's just as if she could read my mind

although hardly ever cruel or unkind.

As I grew older things got worse, she made predictions all in verse!

She must be psychic, that's the clue,

but why in rhyme and rhythmic too?

I said, "Oh hell, why do I bother?

'Cos after all she's still my mother!"

22.10.2014

QUADRANGULATION

Across a crowded room, they say, it only takes a glance,

revisiting that old cliché, the start of a romance.

They knew at once there was no chance, their lives were full beholden

to other partners at the dance , tandem years so golden.

And yet first touch so hesitant, bloomed swiftly into passion,

risks they took concomitant, with suicidal fashion.

There was no limit, not for them, no hour they would not spare,

no rules that might implore for them to cease what they could share.

And so the magic years rolled by, in darkened rooms they clung,

each parting with a stone cold sigh, sour taste upon the tongue.

When finally, she chose to choose the path of safe exclusion,

for him began eternal blues.....this could not be conclusion.

He begged, cajoled, would not believe, their heights were gone forever.

"Say it's over then I'll grieve!" Her sad reply... "could never..."

So there in Limboland they stand, yearn for what they had.

Innocent meetings, calls she'd banned, were those ten years that bad?

12.05.2006

RANDOM RHYME... RANDOM REASON

What does inspire one's writing urge,

a need to scribe becomes a surge.

Communication, pen and ink, or mouse and keyboard, just to think

that waves of creativity, do flood with sensitivity.

Convey ideas with written word from lofty peaks to low absurd...

thus far I've kept to rhythmic rhyme

but need not do so all the time.

So now my spirit floats adrift,

allowing dreams to come alive.

I write without those cast-iron chains

expression free , unburdened mind...

Alas! I must confession make,

what rules there are I dare to break,

depressed to say it lasts not long,

for Rhyming is where I belong!

30.10. 2013

RECIPES FOR DREAMS

Invasion of your peaceful sleeping, what you ate comes slyly creeping...

late, late snack of four- cheese pizza , repeats past midnight when it hits ya!

Reds and yellows all a-twirling, like United Nations flags unfurling.

Dessert divine Meringue Chantilly, haunts your nightmares willy-nilly!

A juicy steak however rare, regurgitates so just beware...

you'll dream of blood and guts, red raw,

your abdomen will feel quite sore,

but yet you'll sleep perchance to dream,while letting out a primal scream!

Too much to drink... your head is hurting,

control with luck your kidneys spurting!

A plate of cheesy cauliflower, dream channel switches every hour!

After eating chicken fear of falling while comatose is quite appalling...

you're up there wingless, flying high, then four a.m. you crash and die!

Those nightly visions so surreal, are consequential from your meal!

The worst is cabbage, take my word, a sleepy sound track will be heard

by whoever's nearest, hear me say, perfumed divorce is on the way!

Late at night 16.10. 2013

REEVA

Four am. Sweltering heat. Pitch dark.
Do I hear noise? From where? Do I imagine it?
Throw off soaking sheet. Clamber towards verandah doors.
Struggle with blinds. Peer into half-lit exterior.
No sign of anyone or anything.
Noise is inside. Cold sweat consuming me. Crawl to bedside.
Grab revolver. Click off safety. Limp towards bathroom.
Toilet door closed. Yell warning but trigger finger itchy.
Fire four shots into door.
Scream from within. Oh God! Turn back to bedroom.
Her side of bed empty.
Oh God! Oh God! "REEVA!" I scream.
Grab cricket bat. Bash open locked toilet door. Blood everywhere.
She lies slumped to one side. Hardly breathing, eyes closed.
Oh God!

*

"You bloody bitch! You whore!
You're sleeping with him, aren't you?
I fuckin' don't believe a word!" She screams.
I swing cricket bat.
Connect with her head. She dashes to bathroom.
I hear toilet door locking.
I ignore my metal legs, grab my revolver.
I'll show her, the unfaithful little slut!
I enter bathroom. I fire three, no four shots. I hear her scream.
I raise the bloodstained bat. I shatter the locked toilet door.
She lies slumped over.
Blood everywhere. I panic. My cell-phone in my hand.
Who to phone?
Better report to Emergency. Then my agent.
He'll know what to do.
He says carry her downstairs.
I do that, thinking his version over and over.
Police come. Reeva dies in my arms. Oh God, what have I done?
Who will the world believe? My agent arrives. He reassures me.
You're The Blade Runner. No need to worry. So that's what I do. I don't worry.
WHICH TO BELIEVE???

27.02.2013

A WHITER SHADE OF PALE

His ashen reflection stared back at him, disbelieving.

Two dark orbs set deep in his narrow face.

Deafening silence after shattering sounds.

Her screams, explosions, clatter of lethal weapon on tiled floor

as his paralysed fingers relinquished their hold.

Redness seeping beneath the locked door. Smell of cordite overwhelming.

Room pitch dark and yet...by vague moonlight he could feel his way...

on amputated stumps back to the bed he knew was empty.

Frenzied panic turned to self-preservation.

Scenario forming rapidly in his tormented mind.

Seeking plausible reason for his raging actions.

Volume of three am altercation must surely have been heard far and wide.

To say nothing of gunshots and her dying moans.

Hands trembling he reaches for his phone..to begin defending his defenceless killing...

of what he believed to be his faithless woman.

05.03. 2014

REFLECTIONS

Those priceless three-score years and ten,

alas! Fair youth will never come again!

When did I first devour that rhyme, and denigrate Old Father Time?

For now beyond that limited age, I dare not turn another page

in fear of what may lie beyond, like reflections in a glassy pond.

The mirror speaks uncompromising, of deepened lines, not so surprising,

of whitened hair, praise be still thick...and silent thanks, I'm not yet sick!

But as each day draws to a close, insomnia haunts each night's repose.

I find myself comparing to... surviving friends, right now so few.

I dare not find religion yet, which God to trust, which way to bet?

Have not yet booked my burial plot, cremation? No I'd rather not!

And so I go my merry way, rejoice to live another day!

Thus when the signs of my decay are clear as glass, you'll hear me say...

I've had enough, just turn me in, my life was full, brim full of sin!

I'll take a flight to Dignitas, no need for prayer not even Mass!

My dusty bones on some fine Alp,

no fires in Hell for my poor scalp!

22.02. 2012

REPRISE ON REFLECTIONS

On second thoughts I might not go , there are other choices as you know.

First's when body's in decline, your brain in cylinder, minus eighty-nine!

Surrounded by ice, white, steamy and then, in millennium use your brain once again!

Alternately using a little glass dish they scrape your skins like scales of fish.

Then nourish, infuse, incubate and grow,

into someone not unlike the person you know.

So with new cryogenics and cell differentiation

you on your own can create a new nation!

Friends, CARPE DIEM because it's no way too sure

that the futuristic you will be entirely pure.

You may end up like that great film The Fly

with eyes out on stalks, six legs all awry,

or nose not too Jewish, twelve fingers and toes,

a tail that resembles your old garden hose!

In conclusion I'll stick with things as they are...

maybe my soul will smile down from a star!

23.02. 2012

ROMANTIC CONCEIT OF FREEDOM

So you think you're free, do you?
I suppose we like to think we are free...
yet everywhere we are in constraints.
Seat belts, helmets, airport body searches,
girdles, corsets, brassieres and yes, jockstraps too!
To be free or not be free?
Hang on a minute, what exactly is meant by freedom?
To wake each day, face the sun, and smile?
Or lie awake throughout the night, afraid of shadows?
Petrified of what each new day will bring?
Feel materialistically secure? Does that really provide freedom?
Is that truly enough? ***When is more enough?***
Freedom to speak one's mind...
anywhere, at any time, to anyone?
Oh yes, hurl insults at any religion except one notable exception...
Stand in protest at injustice...then land in back of a black maria!
Choose a preferred direction...unencumbered?
And what of the ballot box?
The farce they call Democracy!
Your pencilled X means little now.
Pollsters and party politicians rule OK...
Megaton EU blunders atop meekly compliant nations,
depriving us all of true independence.
Government of the People, for the People by the People?
Pull the other one!
Truly a conceit of romantic proportions!
Freedom? I PASS!

26.02. 2014

RUMMAGE

You queue in corral for hours, really quite a scrummage.

No wonder travellers lose their cool and you, well you take umbrage!

You've taken off your shoes and belt, trousers now quite loose.

Put your jacket on a tray, whole thing's quite obtuse!

Computer separate to go thru x-ray, place bag on rolling pins, vanishes same way.

Woman peers at screen, checks for explosive liquid.

Your aftershave she'll confiscate, watch you turn quite livid!

You go through arch God help if you've got metals...

they take you to private room, undress down to your petals!

But worst of all when you've gone thru, they've taken off your luggage,

now Amazon with plastic gloves through all your things will rummage!!!!

Your undies she'll throw aside, your privates she will shake up......

she'll yell out loud 'hey, you're a man what for you need this make-up?'

We know, don't we, who caused this fuss? Why all this mad security?

Those you-know-who's with long black beards wanna bomb us to obscurity!

But in the end they'll let you go, you've probably missed your plane!

The moral of this poem is... You're better off by train!

08.02.2012

SACRIFICE

*A word that carries its meaning beyond pain, immolation of self for
another.
Foregoing worldly goods for a cause.
In days of yore a spiritual cleansing, or pagan ritual to pacify the
deities.
Charitable beings giving their selfless time for the less fortunate.
Yet what can one say about Wafa al-Biss?
Except by cynical rhyme, for this woman transcends the bounds of
decency?*

*

*Returned to Gaza, one of a thousand, exchanged for one Israeli
youth,
Wafa al-Biss proclaimed to children "Martyr's path is Truth!"
Body burned all over, her life saved, by Israeli care and devotion.
Her family wrote to Surgeons in full appreciation.
"The care was wonderful and warm", they said, yet just a few
months later,
heavily clothed, she approached the border, hiding a detonator.
On instructions given by stern masked men, eyes cold as ice,
"Return to hospital with suicide belt! Make Supreme Sacrifice!!!"
Killing those who had helped her and others equally innocent.
Prevented, thank God, from performing this act, rewarding her life-
saving treatment.
How can we understand this Faith, forcing Wafa to don a belt
to reward her healers with instant mass death, some guilt she surely
must have felt?
And then when freed, alive and well, speak to children thus.....
"Walk this path, be martyrs all" what message is there for us?
With folks like these it's certain, appeasement will never suffice!!
For we love Life, and they love Death, they worship Supreme
Sacrifice!*

08.11. 2011

SECRETS OR KEEPING SHTUM

The tip of your rosy-red tongue, a precarious place to be,

when you've just heard something juicy, but were sworn to secrecy...

You realise, that that self-same vow, was asked not just of you but many.

The question is, if that's the case, was this secret just ten a penny?

You've heard of Chinese whispers, how things get overblown....

original's quite out of shape, thanks to accursed mobile phone.

And so when Mrs A lets slip who Mrs B went with last night,

you can be sure, when Mrs C is told, details will be out of sight!

I guess it's more a female thing, to spread and dish the dirt...

'cos probably it's not too often a wife's got a lip-sticked shirt!

Men on the whole are more trustworthy, they know how to keep real shtum,

most likely what they learn from birth, or even while in the womb!

So when you're told a secret and asked, keep your big mouth shut...

don't waste a mo, just let it go, especially if its smut!

09.05.2012

SHADOWS,

We watch as they lengthen

inch by inch consuming

that which once was lit.

The source always behind, darkness ahead.

Folds beneath eyes and jaw

proceed apace,

implacable , unkind.

Legacy left in trust.

Who will recall a man who once lived?

Now mere shadows on a stone.

Yet comes the dawn

new statues in the sunlight

at midday cast no shade.

Their turn will come.

21.03. 2012

SO WHAT'S NEW?

Summertime ending.

Foliage browning.

Autumnal aromas arising.

Chill breezes billowing.

Skies greying.

Joints creaking,

nostrils sniffling, sinuses blocking.

Furry boots appearing.

Fingertips numbing.

Fireplaces smouldering, chimney stacks smoking.

Heating cheques arriving, pensioners freezing.

Windows closing.

Human hibernation beginning.

C'est la vie!

09.10. 2013

SORROW

Ebb and flow of tireless tides, emerging from the depths

come crashing on the shallows.

Frothing, foaming, flattening melting footprints on the sand.

Blackness of the early hours, mind alive with platitudes......

guilt, astir with consternation,

anger, bright and flaming at being misunderstood.

Yet loss repeats, continues,

it's grip tight fast upon the throat.

In vain, glimpse to horizon,

perhaps conflicts with never,

hope receding like the swells.

There can be no mistaking such message plain and clear,

a voice once so familiar

from oceans distant strikes the shore...

a fervent wish to be apart..

forever.

18.01. 2012

STIRRING STUFF

Speeches can be stirring stuff, like sending men to war,

even though they may not know what they are fighting for.

They urge young chaps to conflict, while leading from behind,

blood and guts and glory spent, till peace treaty is signed!

But what of all the folks at home, mums and dads and widows?

Speeches leave them cold, unmoved, while mourning their lost shadows.

Malicious bit of stirring results in marital upheaval.

Casual word that wronged wife heard can be a deadly evil.

A phrase that's meant with good intent destroys connubial bliss.

Inevitable outcome sad but numb, a bitter goodbye kiss.

I once attempted to make fudge, ingredients all in place...

it never set in spite of stirring, till pink and blue in face!

They tell us sugar is no good for you and me,

but damn them, it will never stop two lumps stirred in my tea!

In my conclusion may I say, avoid please stirring stuff...

for as above the loss of love and fudge can be quite rough!

30.01, 2014

THAT TIME OF YEAR

Wind howling, clouds scudding, frost on garden grass...

Skies darkened, cheeks reddened

winter's here at last!

Overcoats buttoned, gloves discovered, furry boots all ready,

mufflers swirling, cold toes curling,

central heating on steady.

Gale force whipping, nostrils dripping, fingertips all numb...

wear several layers say your prayers

hyperinsulate your bum!

I do so love the winter, need never go outside...

just turn the gas fire right up high,

retire to bed and hide!

When someone yells out freeze I rush to get my skates on...

and fly to some near frozen pond...

the ice too thin...I'm gone!

05.12. 2013

THE 6 A.M. POEM

You emerge   from end-lit tunnel.

You become aware   and grow.

You discover   another.

You pair   producing

one, two, maybe three   or two-point-four embryos.

You nurture   you care.

You thrive   you err.

They grow   steadily diverging.

You differ   often bitterly.

One may fly well   one not quite,

one not at all.

You age   you decline.

One may be there   one not quite,

one not at all.

You disappear.......................

11.10. 1997 (rewritten February 2011)

THE AMOROUS PLUMBER

Upon solemn reflection, it's not so surprising,
plumbing profession prone to sudden uprising.
After all they do deal in most rigid of pipe-work...
and quite frequently too he'll be called out for night-work!
Arriving quite late with his wrenches and rods,
saying ' sorry mate' as sundry apertures he prods.

Constantly faced with fluids a-flooding,
thoughts probably laced with male hormones a-thudding!
The lady's distressed, most concerned with the leakage...
he imagines her undressed, can't ignore her cleavage!
For his arrival she's grateful, a woman in panic,
yet his presence is fateful, with reaction volcanic.

Once he's unblocked the blockage, she offers a grin...
he senses advantage, and thinks "Gawd! I'm in!"
He's probably right as so often happens...
her hubby's on nights, or down at the taverns.
Without further ado he's off her and on her,
then a cup of quick brew to assuage her honour!
So Ladies beware, of a plumber named Jason,
he'll like as not clear more than your blocked up basin!

PS Sometimes they're called on to unblock your sewer,
climb down smelly cauldron, any romance to skewer!
Just offer him a shower, with perfumed soap as well...
it's you he'll deflower, then take an oath he won't tell!

30.11.2011

THE BELT OF LIFE

It fits me so snugly, just like a glove,

tailored to measure, from the One God with Love.

There's a little red nipple round like a plum,

a caress is forbidden, but my moment will come.

I'm young, just fourteen, but for certain I know,

my destiny is just, rewards they will flow.

I hide in my room, far from all prying eyes,

repeating my prayers, taught to me by allies.

Last night when they came I was told 'feel the joy

when tomorrow you change into MAN from mere boy!'

So, awaiting a bus, fully cloaked, here I stand,

Imam's words in my heart, deep in Infidel land.

The buckles are tight, my breathing is short,

I survey every face, I must not be caught.

The bus comes, I board, vibrant Virgins not far,

I press the red nipple, shouting 'Allah Akhbar!

14.05. 2003

THE BOTTOM OF THE HILL (1)

Starting point for ambition, only way is up,

end point after failure mere residue of gloom.

Look around contemporaries, compared with you yourself...

are they ascending or downward heading, will your paths cross on the way?

Is life itself about achievement or always losing, coming last?

the oh so very distant summit seems an unattainable goal,

and yet, you summon every fibre to climb, arms outstretched,

just when you think I'm nearly there they smile at you and say...

he surely gave it his best shot .too late ,alas! He's over the hill!

THE BOTTOM OF THE HILL (2)

Starting point for one's ambition, only way is upward,

or end point after failure? Couldn't cut the mustard!

Look around comparing contemporaries with yourself,

do they ascend or downward glide, their lives upon the shelf?

Is life about achievement or losing, coming last?

The very distant summit is receding all too fast.

You summon every fibre to climb, your arms flung wide...

just when you think I'm nearly there, their scorn they try to hide.

He gave it his best shot until he wound up over the hill!

29.10. 2014

THE COMMON TOUCH

You must excuse my age, My Lord,
memory's not what it was.
I regret the victim's rage, My Lord,
it may just be because
I found her rear end shape, My Lord,
so fetching and so plump...
could simply not restrain, My Lord,
my hand upon her rump!
T'was many years ago, My Lord,
but this I can recall...
it wiggled to and fro, My Lord,
just like a bouncy ball!
This here's my wobbleboard, My Lord,
I shake it up and down,
like girls' bottoms I adored, My Lord,
so please My Lord don't frown!
My hit song Jake the Peg, My Lord,
sold millions by the way,
that naughty extra leg, My Lord,
caused more grief than words can say!
I meant no harm at all, My Lord,
just wished young girls to know...
I appreciate rise and fall, My Lord...
Now oh please let me go!

04.06. 2014

THE KNOCKOUT

Seemed to come from deep south-west, saw nothing, a time-delayed snapshot.

Liniment-scented recall, muscled masseur paws tightly taped.

Sequined gown, laced leather pillows.

Emerging from dim-lit dungeon, midst smoke-throttled roar,

pallid Queensberry gladiator, British-born thrusting through patting hands, t-shirt
security.

Brain-splitting cacophony, blinding neon.

Ropes part, dark rippling adversary across resined-canvas ocean.

Penguins strut, PA blaring. gloves touch, eyes glare.

Time concertinas, shapely belles with boards. Distant bells ring.

Nakedly alone, armed with trainer vocals, roadwork long-forgotten, defence,
survival.

Certain knowledge of second place.

He's stronger, younger, fitter. A natural.

I'm just here for the breadwinning.

Never saw it coming. From deep southwest.

An arced rainbow of blooded sweat.

Why has the penguin four faces?

27.03.2001

THE WAY WE LIVE AND DIE

It caught my eye as I passed.

A bunch of withered blooms.

Drooping, loosely tied to lamp-post,

sign of someone mourning.

Our loved one died right here.

Victim of the pace we live,

no matter how hard we try.

We paint our signs, pattern our roadways.

A moment's indiscretion,

second's lack of concentration.

A life is snuffed away.

People grieve and apportion blame.

But it goes on.

And always will.

19.06. 2013

THE WIDOW

"It's just not fair" the woman said, to anyone who'd listen.

"I'm in my prime, body's taut, my clear complexion glistens.

Why did he have to snorkel deep, so far out from the shore?

He knew there would be sharks about, my Hubby tasty for sure!

We'd only recently married, a matter of ten short days.

Slowly I became attuned to his decidedly peculiar ways.

Getting up at 5 am, while I in bed would laze.

He'd do the Telegraph crossword and three Sudokus too,

then come hand me a cup of tea 'fore running off to the loo.

But Underwater was his thing, even snorkelled in the bath....

so when he had the chance at sea, well, you know the aftermath.

The shark removed his hands and feet, and massive chunk of chest.....

now all I'm left are memories not even part of him I loved best!"

01.09. 2011

TIME OF YEAR

It's quarter to four in the afternoon...........

and feels like midnight,

ghostly sun peering spectre-like

just above horizon.

Leafless trees sway silently

beneath birdless blackening sky.

Penetrating chill escapes

in white breathy clouds,

smouldering foliage pervades smoky air.

Irresistible lure of cosy wood fire,

doors closed, curtains drawn,

kettle on.....

December.

09.12. 2014

TOGETHERNESS

You do your thing and I do mine, it's been that way for years.

House is empty without you, I guess you feel so too.

Togetherness personified, with not too many tears.

Now 'empty-nesters' we are called,

we can afford something smaller,

let young folks in, poor dears!

But actually we like it here, we're all paid up, no fears

and when the kids come home, you see

we've space round our armchairs!

So why should we, who've worked our fill, make way for folks who haven't?

This is our home, can't kick us out, it's comfy and it's pleasant!

I realise we'll have to face the dreaded time to come,

when one of us is left alone, to ignore that would be dumb,

or just maybe, we'll have the luck, to share our ills together,

employ one nurse for two of us, no matter what the weather!

Let's hope we'll still be compus mentus, plan our exodus,

private ambulance and plane....... to Switzerland I will march us!

26.10. 2011

UNDECIDED

On the other hand...

always seems to be another hand, doesn't there?

Or maybe not, as case may be.

Inclinations teeter, first one way then t'other.

Attempt to reach decision, consider all the angles.

Conflicting thoughts intruding so return to where you started.

Not sure when it began, this indecisive curse.

Of one thing you are certain, it might be getting worse!

Can't even make your mind up to write free or rhyming verse!

So finally in conclusion,

the fourth and final inning,

In uttermost confusion

I'll go back to the beginning !!!

05.06.2001

VOICES

Silver disc untitled in unlabelled cover,

curiously inserted

in slot provided.

Volume to full...

blurred indistinct sounds...

few piano notes then

voices fondly remembered.

Bygone era,

innocent infant's chorus.

Some now have children of their own.

Plaintive violin followed

by gentle tenor...

my father's voice,

our family's greatest hits.

07.05. 2014

WHAT IF??????

What if we had no sense of smell? Would life be a total sterile hell?

Coffee brewing, bacon a-stewing, none of these would be accruing!

Deodorant sales crash thru the floor...

Perfume counters shown the door from every large department store?

And yet just take a mo to think, what life would be without the stink

of dog-turd stuck beneath your shoe, while no-one looks askance at you?

They all smell nothing now, you see, so enjoy your BO innocently!

There'll be no need for good hygiene, what's the point in keeping clean?

Throw out your useless wash-machine,

just one pair of knickers if you're that mean!

But what if you can't smell the smoke from precious marijuana toke?

You'd go on merrily inhaling, above the ceiling you'd be sailing!

When driving it'll be much later, as steam exudes from radiator!

Savour an odourless experience visiting a public convenience!

When asked by the waiter to whiff the wine

your nostrils won't know just how to decline!

Finally for doting mums, you'll sniff not a thing from cheeky messy bums!

Maybe then you'll wish that you could sense

that uniquest of aromas, so pungent and intense!

So, no, to conclude my non-olfactory rhyme

give me back my big nose each and every niffy time!

27.05.2012
(on board easyJet!)

CRUMBS

Crumbs! I thought uncertainly, which way should I vote?

Red, Blue, Orange or Purple, Green sticks in my throat!

I worry about my country, fast filling to the brim...

but friends say you're a fascist if you dare to vote for him!

So Crumbs! I'm undecided...do I go Posh or Red?

If Nige my vote is wasted... but Ed's in Sturgeon's bed!

I no longer trust the media, the Salmond-pink BBC...

and all the polls are screwed up...was Britain ever free?

TV debates are boring, Dimbleby's lost control,

and now to my amazement... creep Russell Brand's on a roll!

There's just no hope for Blighty, we're on a downward course...

especially now with Nicola, Scotland's unstoppable Force!

So finally I've decided, after weeks of chewing my gums...

I'll spoil my voting paper... and scrawl across it... Crumbs!

30.04. 2015

Election-Day minus seven

(Written at Creative Writing class in 5 Minutes!)

A JEWESS OF TODAY

She stands by the crossroads.

Auburn coils tucked beneath her beret.

She stands, rifle by her side.

Desert coloured uniform, dusty from the roadside.

She waits. Dark eyes gazing into distant mirage.

Waiting for a bus or kindly driver

to return her to her unit.

GENERATION GAME

She never passes a reflective surface without stopping, first to glance

then to admire her eyes of blue, locks of gold. Maya, my daughter's daughter.

Mirrored echoes of the past, the not so long ago.

Sat in a deep chair gazing at her reflected image

whilst hairdo lady permed her blue-gray hair.

Sarah, aka Sadie, my beloved mother.

Sadly, no longer does she gaze at reflections,

or sit hunched in a corner armchair.

Asked nurse for arsenic and waited to die.

Maya will only know her from pictures on our walls,

or painstakingly filled albums......and so it goes.

06.09.06

LOVE

All-pervading, mind and body manacled in its embrace.

Longing always to be nearer, touching, touched, face to face.

Torture to be separated,

fond reunion, breathless bliss.

Savage feuding, happy mending magic of a gentle kiss.

LOSS

Where can they be, those jangling metals without which nothing functions?

No portals widen, nor chests disclose their treasures.

Home is barred, car's at ease,

until I find my fucking keys!

MUSIC

Where have you gone, O Food of Love,

that once adorned our senses?

Now discos, DJ's constant throb...

earplugs are our defences!

Odd Bedfellows 1998

A PHONE CALL

A quickened heartbeat

at the sound of a familiar voice

not heard for so many years.

Gasping intake of breath,

a hesitant response..how to react

to such a longed-for contact?

With warmth, delight, yet guarded with concern,

questioning the circumstance leading to this moment.

Doubts cast aside, father's practicalities uppermost.

"I'll get you home...sit tight!"

Then, a few mind-tormented hours later

she stands at our door,

smiling, but uncertain.

28.11.2014

A VIEW FROM MY ROOM

Like foaming frenzied fedayeen they hurl themselves

in series after series of suicidal salvoes

'gainst impenetrable rock-hard ramparts

only to be repulsed, shamefully receding,

gathering strength for yet another vain onslaught...

whilst above sit I, sipping coolest of martini's,

watching this most uneven of contests as foam turns to yellow phlegm...

thin-necked kelp peacocks poke puny stalks through the brine,

and I content myself with my secure vantage...

although with one almighty leap

I could be enmeshed in this eternal struggle,

no doubt shredded against the barnacles

encrusting these time-outlasting rocks....

I think I'll keep the hotel window shut!

Bantry Bay South Africa 05.04. 2013

A ROW OF BOTTLES

They stood in a line on the edge of his table,

a row of glass bottles filled with drugs to enable

his mood to go up or to bring him right down!

Some to bring smiles, chase away a deep frown...

Bottle of water that'll help him to swallow.

Bottle of gin in self-loathing he'd wallow.

A bottle of perfume to negate BO sweating,

watching the races forget which horse he's betting!

A bottle of aspirin to cure all his headaches,

and bottle of instant for plentiful tea breaks!

He's alone at his table

with essentials in bottles.

As he drains the last one

arse over tit the man topples!

23.06. 2011

BITTERNESS

Ambition dulled, bridges burned,

at crossroads once one might have turned

a different way, to gold, instead,

a doorway home, a cardboard bed.

SILENCE

When all the anger has subsided,

guilt and accusation aired,

when nothing's left but separation

dead silence 'twixt two people shared.

WILDERNESS

Civilisation non-existent,

no roads or pylons to be seen.

Just greenish nature all persistent,

land and ocean lie serene.

Odd Bedfellow 1998

DESERT

Scorching dust, mirage images,

heat to scour the innards of one's skull.

Blurred horizons, stunted bush,

red rock ravaged by the sun.

DESOLATION

Alone he stands outside the Doctors,

stunned to silence by the news.

Alone to face a shortened future,

enough to give a man the blues.

Odd Bedfellows 1998

CROWS KNOW

Thud in cold fireplace. Cloud of black dust.

Movement so slight.   A mournful eye in the dark..

Motionless feathered torso lifted gently, still breathing. Placed beneath trees.

Sudden cacophony. Sky blackened. Crows a-plenty .Gazing down from treetops.

Their stricken fellow had breathed it's last .Mournful dirge.

Crows' final funereal. Shallow grave. Skies clear.

Crows know.

A TIME OF LONGING

Fleeting years do not dim his memory.

I see his face in crowded places.

Pictures of him adorn my walls.

A life cut short, leaving behind a haunting smile,

and my reminiscing.

If he were here today, how would it be?

Would we be close as we were?

Brothers laughing, daring, gallivanting,

knowing, anticipating each other,

as well as can be for two separate beings?

A last poignant farewell kiss upon a forehead cold as stone.

Calendar dates, musical themes evoke

emotions, vivid images, filling me

with longing for what was,

and is no longer.

05.06. 2013

A MONOLOGUE WITH HASHEM
(or entreaty of a modern-day Noah)

Forgive me, O Lord, I'm confused,
of Heresy I may be accused.
So often thy name's been abused,
please understand why I am so bemused.
You have so many aliases it's ludicrous,
whilst those imitating you are insidious.
Adonai or Jahweh, for the fastidious,
Heavenly Father sounds just right, it's melodious!
To begin there were heathens with many gods.
Golden idols were ten-for-a-penny gods.
Atheists won't accept there are any gods!
Politicians sometimes think they are demi-gods!
In the beginning you were known as Jehovah
then the Mount Sinai Jews turned you over.
Moses's Tablets put them right post-Passover
Jesus' Christians then launched a takeover!
So Oy Vay! There's a Son! Holy Ghost!
contesting who could convert the most!
Mohammed's Allah was the toast
Islam spreading from desert to coast!
They call you the God of Great Mercy
Please explain this annoying controversy...
If eye-for-eye tooth-for-tooth is your policy
Then please God no more Political PC!
Your alter ego the Devil Incarnate
you desire above all to eliminate.
Great Satan indeed is some reprobate,
but nice balance between you is too delicate!
When you look down upon your Creation
wear a frown as nation fights nation.
Are you tempted to express exasperation
thinking seriously about extermination....?
Please God may I make a suggestion?
Before you take action in question,
if I say a long Brocha, will you save my Mishpocha
and while you're at it, cure my indigestion?

06.09.2011

AFTER THE RAIN

Will grey clouds part as usual?

Will mown grass smell sweeter than usual?

Will our sun ever shine once more?

Can there be reprieve from storm of silence?

Hearts leap with joy on loving reunion?

Does chasm of estrangement bear seeds of renewal?

Surely rainbow's golden end foretells joyous welcome return?

My earth is damp, more than sufficient

from tears that fall each day.

It's time for hope to swell,

begin again, once more.

After the rain.

07.09.2011

"DRINK, MY DARLING?"

Ah! Champagne served

in cut-glass frosted flute, round rim coated

with glistening whiteness.

Crystalline melting at sensual lips touch,

dispensing delicate sweetness.

Accompanying bubbles assault the senses...

tongue greedily licking few remaining grains.

"Recline...let fruit of the vine

work it's mischief.

Your very good health,

my darling girl!"

"Thank you, yours too...

Sugar Daddy Dearest!"

29.05. 2013

AN ENCOUNTER

(or two days and nights on the southern seas)
In the distance, pensively, receding harbour wall,
I could see them, my parents, youngest brother, so tall.
They waved, I waved, they became just mere specks
on dusky horizon, as we few craned our necks.
Two days to Durban with no stops in between,
hardly any aboard our luxury liner serene.
We stood at the railings, a vicar and wife,
a tearful young woman, and me, eager for life.
That evening, Captain's table, we all met to dine,
she shared her sad tale over many glasses of wine.
Her age thirty-five, twelve years my senior,
attempting to assuage a long romance's failure.
In Durban she'd meet him, her too-Jewish lover
ten hide-away years, protecting his mother.
A make-or-break voyage, to decide on their future
but she'd more or less decided their affair was pure torture.
So there I sat listening, myself on rebound
from similar situation, sympathy quite profound.
We drank and we danced, then drank even more.
When the band packed it in we staggered out door...
with the moon shining bright on the calm Southern Seas
we kissed and romanced with consummate ease.
"There's a girl in my cabin," she gasped, up for air...
"There's no girl in mine, the four bunks all are bare,"
said I with a laugh, "you're welcome, I'm sure!"
Hand-in-hand she murmured, "You could be my cure!"

So for forty-eight hours our bodies entwined
apart from the few when with Captain we dined!
We loved, laughed and cried, who knew what next day would bring
when our cabins would fill, bring an end to our fling.
In those long-ago days only married folks shared
so she had three women, me three guys.... who cared?
Two were my mates with whom I was travelling
and an unknown , Mr Cohen. Was my libido unravelling!
When they all came aboard in Durban that day,
my love and I watched, trying hard to be gay...
but imagine my chagrin, when I learned that this Cohen
was my sweetheart's fiancé, with him on tour she was goin'!
Sharing my cabin which had seen such romantics
with this middle-aged bloke, no more fancy antics!
Next three weeks we spent sailing Africa's east Coast,
but our sense of frustration was what I remember the most!
Apart from occasional lingering looks,
we never again exchanged any physical hooks.
As I write this down now, fully fifty years on,
I shiver recalling that lost love long gone!
I met Mr. Cohen a few years ago.
He wanted to punch me, but then let it go.
He told me, Elise, for that was her name,
became a nun, forsaking fortune and fame.
So our passionate encounter rests tender in my brain,
and I'm saddened that we never met up again!

29.02. 2012

CROATIA

I stand alone on deck in wonderment.

Behold a glassy calm ocean frilled by scurrying shoals beneath.

Silence save for sail above me, sensual hiss as prow bisects the swell.

Horizons distant gently swaying, evening sun slowly sinks

midst reddened sky overseeing darkest blue.

Dolphins play alongside, smile as they pass

behind, below, ahead, whilst all the while

mocking us, land-locked interlopers with glorious nautical manoeuvres.

The wind grows, sails fill,

Persil-white sea- horses parade before each strengthening gust.

Seeking shelter from the black of night, a merciful haven for anchor to fall,

and, sail safely stowed, comes sleep, a rhythmically rocking rest,

hearing only gentle gurgle

of crystal water 'gainst welcoming wharf.

14.07.2008

BARBARIANS AT THE GATE

They march down streets,
a seething mass of humanity,
mouthing inane slogans,
waving sinister black flags.

Arms raising rifles to the sky.
Faces wreathing, contorted with hate.
Triumphant turban-headed troops
on machine-gun-bearing trucks
spreading their archaic barbarism.
Striding through wrecked buildings,
they demolish even historic ancient sites.

Helpless innocents flee
dragging infants, meagre belongings
to a hope-filled safer haven.
Where will they stop?
When their desert lands are sated
with primitive belief and chaos...
will they set their sights
on our green fields?

20.07.2014

BENDING THE RULES

There are Rules that are meant to be broken, and Laws that should be observed.

The difference betwixt these two boundaries is greyness for gamblers reserved.

When driving does one halt at a stop sign or proceed at a pace as one pleases?

Ignoring the oncoming truckload and its driver's frenetic yell......
JESUS!

Freeway limits should generally be exceeded, everyone else does so why should you differ?

Except when speed cameras you anger, the penalties might well become stiffer!

Accumulate ASBOS a-plenty, the Courts hand those out in abundance......

young yobbos rejoice in offending, the Judges' stern words mere encumbrance.

One goes through one's life law-abiding, then sees all around mass defection,

from accepted and proper behaviour, above all avoiding detection.

Young maidens get flats from the councils by using repeated deflowering.....

never minding the number of daddies, on them handouts and benefits are showering!

If you want to get right up my nostrils please don't mention those scoundrels political...

in a league on their own in Westminster, very top of the range hypocritical!

Bogus mortgages, house flippers, they're the worst of the lot...

false expenses, duck houses, they don't give a jot!

Bush and Blair, what a pair, weapons of mass destruction...

in 'sexing up' dossiers didn't need no instruction!

Good old-fashioned customs have disappeared willy-nilly.....

Don't like four letter words? You're told "Don't be silly!"

Obscene pictures, violence, fraud and dishonesty,

atheism, religion, same sex and immorality,

Just keep bending the rules, it's not so hard to bear...

if you don't you'll be labelled a Reactionary Square!

17.11. 2011

BINMANIA

(or....Brown bin, Blue bin, where the hell 'ave you bin?)

Once every week, maybe right by the clock

the bin men arrive and it is quite a shock,

the fact that these guys even turn up at all

so please do make sure that you OBEY their call!

Brown for all things perishable.

Left-over food, rotting vegetable.

Penalty's payable if lid's not properly closed,

all the bin's contents left out in the road!

Blue's for paper and plastic and stuff,

tin cans, wine bottles should be quite enough...

green bin's for all of the other refuse

not blue or brown, even old worn-out shoes!

Beware of microchip stuck in the lid,

nasty bin men will know something wrong that you did...

in which case you've had it

forever and a day...

pay the fine or your garbage

in your garden will stay!

03.10.2012

BLOOM

Dear Reader, the topic for today is BLOOM,

but I'm quite allergic to flowers in my room...

with stamens, pistils, birds and bees

I am most certainly ill at ease.

Floral tributes are not my scene,

Literal or figurative whatever those two do mean!

I don't do perennials, perish the thought!

Arum lilies at funerals leave me totally distraught!

I disregard the BLOOM on my lover's fair cheek

or a BLOOMing red abscess with inflamed boils that reek.

My journey just blossoms....it merely entails..

from BLOOM's Kosher restaurant to NY BLOOMingdales!!!!

Both these establishments opened many years ago,

one sold dresses, the other hot salt beef to go..

in New York it was Lexington and 59th Street..

in London's East End BLOOM's latkes were a treat!

Our Queen shopped at BLOOMingdales, celebrities all came..

Film stars and Presidents, they flocked there just the same...

while Whitechapel waiters said " OY! sit there and wait!...

... consider it a mitzvah if you get a clean plate!"

'All Cars to BLOOMingdales' the slogan they sold,

first designer shopping bag if Google truth be told....

With BLOOMS gehakte herring and cold gevilte fish

BLOOMS would gehak any damn thing that you wish!

So while BLOOMingdales store is still going strong,

sad to say once-famous BLOOMS is now really gone ....

No kosher meatballs, chicken soup, beef on rye

Golders Green no pickled herrings, no matter how hard you try!

In conclusion please accept my apologetic gloom

to have strayed far from subject of today ie BLOOM...

But kinderlach, may I tell you

from the bottom of my tochus....

My BLOOMin wife's chopped liver

gives me heartburn but lotsa nachus!!!!!

04.06.2012

BURIED TREASURE

(A despicable rhyming dialogue for mother and boy)

Mother: Oh don't do that, it's quite disgusting,

your index finger upwards thrusting

into your nostril then rotating

is obscene and irritating!

Boy: Oh Darling Mommy... I am so sorry.

It's my blocked nose that makes me worry.

Don't know what's up there, got to measure,

maybe I'll find some buried treasure!

Mother: You're being stupid! Such bad behaviour

to pick your nose then taste the flavour!

Blow your hooter in these tissues,

and please don't show off that which issues!

Boy: Oh mum its fine, I'm feeling clearer...

my nose is clean, relief is nearer!

I promise I won't do this again...

I'll use my thumb, will tell you when!

22.03. 2012

BY THE SEA

Oh I do like to deal beside the seaside,

I do love to sell my LSD...

I do love to flog my drugs beneath the prom

where addicts inject then on the sand they bomb!

Whatever they want I aim to sell them,

be it meths, heroin or crack cocaine...

I come back home a wealthy man, to all junkies I'm a fan

to the seaside, I'll come again!

There's so many prostitutes beside the seaside...

you can bet that all of them will know my name!

They strut up and down along the pier at night,

showing what they've got ... blimey quite a sight!

The tarts are by far the best of clients...

they spend their hard-earned cash on what I sell...

they come to me in pairs, begging me to try their wares...

would I touch them? Like bloody hell!!!

By the seaside you can smell the marijuana...

get on your arse while smoking grass or ecstasy...

from the cliff you throw your spliffs into polluted ocean

and your world is in a whirl of drug induced slow motion!

Oh I profit from the vomit in the arcades...

all the youngsters want to try my coloured pills...

so that when I get back home, far from sand and sea and foam

I miss the seaside and all its thrills!!!

27.09. 2013

CHILDHOOD

Siren wails across clear blue sky.

I run, fast as my seven-year-old legs will carry me.

Into depths of our concrete shelter.

Steel door, window shutters slammed shut.

We wait, strain to hear and feel inevitable shuddering explosion.

It comes, some distance away.

Relieved we smile, mother, sisters, playmates,

as we exit our tiny dungeon.

Saved yet once more...to play in the garden, until the next time.

*

I do not cheer when white-plumed rocket flies toward the heavens.

Others do, wave black flags in ecstasy.

I run, I know what is coming.

They, my brothers, family, friends, stand on rooftops or on the street.

Just as they have been ordered, as if they are hypnotised.

I run, there is no place to hide.

Perhaps in rubble of an already destroyed building.

My world explodes around me.

Screams, whining ambulance sirens fill choking dust-filled air.

Today is my seventh birthday and I have lost both my legs.

In my semi-conscious world I see another boy.

Playing safe in the sun, somewhere to the north.

And I wonder why our childhood differs in such dramatic fashion.

As I breathe my last breath.

04.08.2014

CONTAINED IN SPACE AND TIME ??

Universe indeed, oh how can it be?

With Professor Steve Hawkings I just can't agree.

He says Big Bang was the start of it all,

but I'm sorry his contentions are due for a fall.

If the word Universe means infinite space

then how can it expand, he's right off his face!

Into what can it grow if there's really no limit?

The best I can say of his theory...just bin it!

And why should there ever be beginning and end?

This overblown notion drives me right round the bend!

I have no real problem, philosophically speaking,

in conceiving no boundaries, his misconceptions I'm tweaking.

Our Universe extends beyond infinite realms

in time space dimensions my belief overwhelms!

So the title I chose "Contained in Space and Time"

Is as wrong and error-prone as me writing this rhyme!

19.01. 2012

DOMESTIC DENTAL DRAMA

Hey Mommy dearest, look my front tooth is out!
I 'm not surprised, honey, way you pulled it about...
But Mummy dear, why is there just so much blood?
It's a soggy red mess and, ugh! Like a flood!
Don't worry, honey, blood you've got plenty more...
But mummy I'm worried, it's not even sore!
You're so very brave, my darlingest girl...
let me have a quick look...wow! it's like the tiniest pearl!
Now as it's your first, you are very very lucky
Tooth Fairy will reward you for being so plucky!
Under your pillow tonight your tiny tooth goes...
when you wake in the morning, my sweetness, who knows?
But Mum is the Fairy an Angel with wings
or a goblin with long pointy ears and weird things?
And Mummy, what if I stay awake all the night...
will the Tooth Fairy then get such a big fright?
Also what if I get up to go make a wee
will the Fairy get cross if she doesn't see me?
And what will be under my pillow if she comes...
sweeties or money or pink bubble gums?
Not sweeties or gum, they're so bad for your teeth...
just look under your pillow to see what's beneath!
Now dear, enough questions, wrap tooth in cotton wool
and put your head on your pillow it's so nice and cool...
in the morning you'll wake to a lovely surprise!
But Mum my big sister told me it'll be you in disguise!
And it's all so much bullshit and huge whopping lies!
Go to sleep now immediately, you wise-ass daughter of mine!
Night, Night, Mummy, ten pound note will be fine!

Kiss Kiss!

27.09.2014

THE GIRL WITH THE MOBILE PHONE

Oblivious to all who surround her,

who walk past her.

Unconcerned, she sways,

head inclined,

an instrument hard-pressed to her ear.

Her mouth moves,

eyes alight,

then sadden, lips pursed.

In her life

a crisis?

Or trivial affair ending?

I will never know.

She turns the corner,

out of sight.

Out of my life.

Loss of signal.

March 2001

THE GIFT

When I was a Dentist, many, many years ago,

I had a Persian patient, a Colonel, don't you know.

Whenever he arrived, never empty-handed,

best Beluga Caviar on reception desk had landed.

The stories he would tell me, of downfall of the Shah,

the Sawak Secret Service, of which he was a star.

He managed to escape from the mad Iranian Mullahs...

and came to swinging London Town with many million dollars!

His gold teeth he demanded be changed to porcelain quick...

price was not a problem, yellow smile made him sick!

One day my Colonel turned up, with flat tin of Pistachios.

"Fresh" he said, "from Teheran, salty not like Cheerios!"

Caviar was out of stock, these nuts his gift to me,

for this I did his scale and polish, for nothing, yes for free!

So late that eve when I come home, relax to watch the telly,

I sit in dark brown TV room, get rumblings in my belly.

I open tin and watch the box, eat pistachios by the dozen...

I fall asleep, my wife comes in, says "Hey, the TV's buzzin'!"

She asks me "Darling, what the hell ...white spots on our brown wall?

And next you on the sofa, wow! Them white things they can crawl!"

She switch on light, I look in tin, pistachios not alone...

white weevils I been eatin', my tummy gives a groan!

My wife she says "Don't worry, hon', its all good protein stuff..."

I look at all them maggots, boy, my insides do feel rough!

So now when I see Colonel come for extraction or for filling

I make quite sure my needles blunt and quadruple my billing!

FUTURE PROOFING

Had a thought last night, not sure from where it came.

Stuck with me throughout today...

yesterday a day of albums gazing at parade of years,

lost in reverie, watching growing faces.

Images of generations passed...then it came to me...

Once you're a parent

you're the ghost of your children's future.

03.09.2015

LOOKING DOWN

Looking down upon one's fellow man,

an attribute not to be defended.

It undermines one's self-esteem

although opposite to what's intended !

All are brothers beneath the skin...

that's what one is urged to believe.

Yet our manifestly diverse world

makes it difficult to conceive.

So I go my way, try reconcile

the Hatred and the Love...

killers and the rescuers

all praying to Whatever's Above.

I'm not quite sure where it will end,

as Powers ebb and flow,

declaring, screaming, "Our God's the One!

All Infidels must go!"

14.10.2015

PRACTICE GETS RESULTS

If you practice to perfection

you can win any election.

For instance its absorbin' watching lefty Jeremy Corbin!

He forgot to mention Europe's Federal teeth

that chubby foolish yachtsman Edward Heath!

No-one could ever match her, 'Iron Lady' Margaret Thatcher!

Or become a millionaire like ' honourable' Tony Blair!

Weird mysterious melodrama surrounding Obie H Obama!

With unions hand-in-hand got elected Milliband!

Persistent practice finally crowned that Scottish bore old Gordon Brown!

Economic lack of Practice palls

and did for chubby Edward Balls!

But Eton Sunlight finally shone on our PM Dave Cameron!

The moral of this poem for sure...

Practice! Practice! Try once more...

perfection's just beyond the door!

02.09.2015

PRACTICE MAKES PERFECT

Doctors, Dentists, Lawyers and such, commence their careers as mere amateurs,

put up their shingles which boast their degrees, but in fact they're mere novice contractors!

They ooze self-belief...it's just a facade, they're nervous like first day at school,

if you're their first client or patient quite ill, watch them sweat a lot just to keep cool!

They need guinea pigs to work on, try out their unpractised skills,

they'll blind you with science or what the law says, and prescribe many visits and pills!

On through the years of error and trial they'll hone their abilities quite keen...

till age does require time to retire when perfection is there to be seen!

If you are unlucky to be there at the start, and suffered their errors unknowing...

quite apart from the bills and uncurable ills you'll have law-suits and toenails in-growing!

The remedy, my friends, is to seek middle-age, a professional who is half-way to perfect...

he's practised a while and developed some style, but maybe his results are not suspect!

First check his CV, get referrals and see, if some clients are sick or in jail...

ask him straight to his face, put him right in his place,

how many times sir, this year did you fail???

If you are ever in doubt, just get up and walk out,

don't ever be slow to reject...

by the way here's my card, it won't be too hard,

come see me 'cos I'm practised and perfect!

03.09.2015

THE FIVE SENSES

Without sight you can't see,

without hearing you're deaf...

how cruel of the Cockneys

to call you Mutt and Jeff!

Without smell you will always

miss onions being fried,

if your taste buds are absent,

you'll shovel rubbish inside!

Unable to feel with the tips of your fingers,

sensation of memories is all that just lingers.

Each part of your body

quite numb everywhere...

might as well optimise you can still shed a tear!

Only one option left, just lean back and propose

to get a job as a waxwork

in Madame Tussauds!

28.04.2014

WHISPERS

Whispers was my password I used it all the time.

When seated at computer and accessing on line.

At my great age 'twas easy, remembering just one word...

but recent alterations have made things just absurd!

You gotta have letters and numbers, sometimes eight or nine or ten...

often with my shaky fingers I must enter it again and again!

My Mother's maiden name they want...what next her vital stats?

What kind of pets she favoured? Dogs or mangy cats?

With credit cards I'm hopeless, trying to recollect my PIN...

cashiers are so impatient, seem to think I'm soaked in gin!

As for telephone call centres, far-east accent's bad enough....

but even with both my deaf aids in, understanding a word is rough!

So now I'm through with struggling, all credit cards I've binned...

Given all my cash away, repenting for times I've sinned.

Hired a financial adviser, he'll run my life for me...

look after my portfolio, at last I will be free...

I'm told my old age pension and benefits won't go far

So I'm selling up my mansion...and getting rid of my Rolls Royce car!

01.03.2011

A WRITER'S PROSETTE

I can only write when I'm smoking.

Problem is I gave up smoking at age eleven.

So instead I became a Dentist.

This meant I could only smoke between patients.

But I wasn't smoking then at all.

So I spent 45 years of my life filling teeth, and not smoking.

Now I'm a retired dentist, so I can write again.

Hallelujah! I can smoke again.

Right next to my PC I have an enormous humidor.

Full of cigars which I'm not allowed to smoke in the house.

That's my problem...how to write a novel at the bottom of the garden.

In England when it's raining, WHEN I CAN'T EVEN LIGHT MY CIGARS!

So now you have my history, my previous profession, my addiction and my marital situation.

Please buy my new novel, the price of cigars is rocketing.

It's called 'Nicotine or Dentine', a Dentist's Dilemma.' .(just kidding!)

PS How d'you get cigar ash out from the keys of your PC?

PPS I can write poetry too.... Smoking a hubble-bubble

with plenty apple tobacco,

no weed, that's the trouble

but do you think this blog is wacko?

(dedicated to the late Eric Donner, brilliant writer and good friend who originated the 'Prosette 'format)

PAPERWORK 2

(Try a little tenderness lyricist Ira Gershwin?)

It's so damn dreary, brain-cells get quite weary

of those final demands I can't shirk...

an income tax query, I'm so sick of Paperwork!

It's irritating, piles of bills awaiting payments that drive me beserk.

Bureaucracy I'm hating, my God I loathe this Paperwork!

I know it's quite fundamental, filling forms makes the world go around...

all in triplicate... it's just too intricate...in documents I'm being drowned.

Let's make it safer, ban pen and ink and paper,

computers we'll consign to the murk...

just take it easy, retire and never ever work.

My desk is overflowing, paper-shredder's on the blink,

I think I'll shoot the postman, and pour myself another drink...

I won't continue, ignore the Inland Revenue demands for tax I'll delay with a smirk...

and when they come to get me I'll blame it on the paper work!

In jail I'll weave my baskets, make paper-machet caskets and

with joyous pride show off my handiwork...

I never pleaded guilty, I blamed it on the paper work!

Friends it's all so easy, just blame it on the paper work!

09.10.2014

ALIEN BLOOD

Streaming down the ages, infecting as it goes.
Corrupting and disfiguring, like sulphurous lava flows.
Ignoring righteous morals,
of decent folk like us...
just bursting through our ethics...
evil dark- yellow pus!
Black-draped figures strutting,
screaming hate and fury...
proclaiming their intention of
beheading all world Jewry!

26.11.14

ODOUR OF HAMAS

With their impotent phallic symbols
sending plumes of sterile sperm-trails,
streaking across blue middle-eastern skies...
or spots of light in darkest night.
They are unaware, nor do they care
where orgasms of their hatred land.
Rejoicing in discomfiture of their neighbours,
who scurry at siren call to concrete safety...
not so their own brethren...
mere fatal fodder for international tears!
Excrement of their rocketry as wasted
as lives of their 'martyrs',
waiting in vain for eternally promised nubile virgins!
The world sits by quietly immovable,
in face of a scourge which knows no boundaries.
You have been warned!

Mike Davidson in Israel 16.07.14

MY BEST ASSET

My asset quite iconic a sense of the sardonic. a tendency to satirise and mock the moronic!

Achieve jeering laughter at my victim's expense,

especially when there's no-one who will leap to their defences!

Just try and get a word in with bearded Jerry Corbyn,

much hot air from Tony Blair... truth he'd be avoidin'!

Call me Dave will never play Piggy in the Middle...

while most of our esteemed MP's are always on the fiddle!

Anyone drive a bargain like a Diesel-powered Volkswagen,

polluting our atmosphere with nitrous oxide toxin?

Maybe this is Herr Hitler, attacking from the grave...

so return all German motors and our Planet you might save!

Now flooding Europe a million mainly Muslims...and-I'm-certain many thousands more...

welcomed open arms by Angela Merkel's ample busloms (sorry!)

but who the hell is gonna keep the score?

Please don't let it worry ya if they keep bombing Syria,

it worked well in Afghanistan, Iraq and also Libya!

Putin and Obama, tho I'm not their greatest fan...

please don't take the chance of deals with Teheran!

For crying out loud beware the mushroom cloud...

you'd best be bombing pre-Nuclear Iran!

Apologies to Tom Lehrer(MLF LULLABY) 30.09.2015

SINGULAR STATISTIC

Semi-silent V8 thrum, new-hide pungent.

Macho throttle opened wide, solar-plexed exhilarant.

Miles fly as graven black foursome caress concrete-slabbed way.

Citrus strobing through mist gentle FM soothes.

Emerald dials glowing, twin red-eyes magnify.

Life, Time, slowing...

Movement! Sudden!

Rubbery reek, steel screeching, above is below!

All is noise, all is silent, black yet piercing white.

Oblivious clarity, sensational numbness.

Cloying FM continues,

gasoline dewdrops dripping...

Voices...Limbs...Claret flowing freely...

Mine??

January 2000

CHALLENGE

I can feel it down deep at the base of my gut.

All my instincts are sharp, my mind's in no rut.

I'm sweating a little, still there's always Right Guard,

but I'm hating the tension with my nerves straining hard.

Can I perform? Can I manage? To do what I ought?

Why with inadequate feelings are my grey cells so fraught?

It's sure not beyond me, I've done it before,

I faced down my critics and performed loud and sure.

But this time it's different and its making me cringe.

Anyone who well knows me knows I'm not one to whinge.

As a retiree dentist I can face a syringe.

I thought a solution was to buy booze and binge,

but thought of words slurring made my conscience unhinge.

Before such august society that would surely infringe....

so till wee early hours I tried hard to scavenge

rhymes to read in my contribution called Challenge!

0 3.08. 2011

DAY BY DAY BY DAY

Patience they say is a virtue,

at no time was a statement more true...

each day you must wait for improvements,

feel regret when there are but a few...

optimism rises then falls,

despairing if good result palls...

falling asleep proving tricky,

waking and climbing the walls!

No matter if issues are single,

or several dilemmas co-mingle,

self-same requirements applying,

small chance of success brings a tingle!

And so with each peak and trough vying,

to gain uppermost, no want of trying...

teeth gritted, hands clenched, you survive,

as the hours, days then weeks fast go flying!

17.12.14

DISCOVERY

It wasn't in your head before, your wildest imaginings...

didn't have it in you, something you'd never expected,

exploding from hidden recesses.

Sudden surfacing, something new.

Never once in all years past could you have plucked the courage,

of that you are quite certain.

Reaction now, extreme as this capability beyond belief.

Yet as you look, deeper still, what makes you what you are...

comes a smile, a knowing grin memory of some dream...

'All before you knelt and prayed, mightily you stood aloft.

Inhibitions gone to dust, shyness full departed.'

Now awake you feel it still...can this be true?

It's yours right now, the shackles lost...

fear no longer, doubt no more,

discovering the power you lacked...

The Art of Public Speaking!

13.03.2013

THE LIFT

The doors closed, just him and me...

silence between us deafening.

His eyes were piercing, silver hair swept back,

atmosphere quite threatening.

The doors opened. No-one got in.

Disheartening. Frightening.

He reached out a hand, I crouched back in terror.

Quite petrifying.

The lift stopped, doors stayed shut...

my entire body sweating.

I reached out, pressed the red button...

Nothing happening.

He moved toward me,

wearing a villainous smile...

'Which floor darling?'

The doors opened...

Fourth floor! Ladies Lingerie! Underwear! Toilets!

I ran.

07 .05.2015

THE LIST

Write it all down, she insisted.

So I did.

I made a list.

Of sins I'd committed.

Of lies I'd told.

Of nasty things I'd done.

Of resolutions I'd broken.

Of appointments made and not kept.

Of friends I'd treated badly.

Of lesser mortals I'd bullied.

Of wives I'd divorced.

Of taxes I'd avoided.

My pen ran out of ink.

Flushed list right down the sink,

whereupon I went and sacked my Shrink!

29.04.15

MY GREATEST FEAR

Isn't it queer and so hard to bear.. gives one a fright, keeps me up half the night!

That terrified feeling sets one's pulse rate a-reeling...

You just cannot hide it, can hardly abide it!

Feel your gut tighten, nostrils do whiten,

hands start to shiver as double chins quiver!

Sane logic defying, beyond endless trying

to curb this mad terror.. have you made a bad error?

Committed a sin? Don't you know where you've bin?

Or who you were with, was it all just a myth?

Can't remember a thing, were you having a fling?

There's blood on your shirt, mixed with lipstick and dirt...

big lump on your head, your heart's filled with dread...

it's like living a dream, you just wanna scream!

Maybe tell your wife, swear blind on your life last night was a blank, just try being frank!

Who's that at front door, looks like three cops or more?

Please let me wake up, I've drained dry the cup!

I'll now shed a tear, for my worst ever fear is losing my timing

and my talent for rhyming!

01.07.2015

MIXING THE SENSES

Here I sit, swaying in rhythm, huge earphones covering both ears...

bottom quite comfy on cushioned desk-chair,

sun through window warming skin of passing years.

From kitchen aroma of coffee a- brewing, music deafening, penetrating my brain...

messy ashtray sited close beside me...

stale dead cigar-smell pollutes room yet again!

Before my eyes my laptop screen sits vacantly mocking, staring, waiting

for inspiration, not arriving..despite booze, pills, supposedly ego-inflating?

Rumbles emanate from lower abdomen...

surely can't be hunger, just had lunch!

But mouth is dry, so go to fridge..get fizzy drink and crisps to munch!

Suddenly sky outside clouds over..this escapist cell grows sombre, darker...

threatening my intentions to dull,

so I don old faithful tattered parka....

As if by magic I am transformed!

With cloth I clear varifocal lenses,

arthritic fingers tap keyboard non-stop...

behold! I've succeeded in mixing my senses!

06.05.2015

GIDDY MOMENT

She sipped her drink but once, then yet again once more...

My God, it tastes so good, she then gulps an encore.

He does look very nice, perhaps sort of OK,

he's actually very generous,

insists, "No, dear I'll pay!"

She's now drained a full glass, vision's becoming blurred...

bar lights coalesce,

whereupon she downs a third!

Her barstool seems to rotate, head nods to and fro...

(her head nearly nods right off)(if he's Jewish)

He grunts and lifts her torso...

"OK sweetheart off to sleep you go."

(I know where you can schloff)(if he's Jewish)

But waking early next morning...a headache to start the day...

'Gee Whiz! Just one giddy moment,

and the bastard's had his way!'

11.06.2015

EPITAPH TO JIM

6 feet below lie remains of Jim Savile,

BBC's fallen hero, reputation unravelled.

Non-stop revelations by females a-plenty,

all were under-age nymphets, number now more than twenty!

Coming out of the woodwork, a dead DJ to damage,

even one in her eighties, there's not one more savage!

Their memories intact, of mammaries fondled,

nether regions invaded or merely mishandled!

This straw-haired pop-icon now cold in his grave,

lies accused by these dollies who were never too brave

to cry rape at the time, he was famous you see...

earning millions for charity and of course BBC!

Their testimony shows, Jim far more than fixed it,

with numerous nubiles our Jim surely mixed it!

Considering all this here's my proposition...

exhume dear old Jim , let him face Inquisition?

on flight from Israel 06.10.2012

FASHION

Who'd want to be a follower of fashion?

Keep up with the latest of fads...

I choose what I wear without passion...

my Wife says I should just wear my Dad's!

Your teeth and your smile are important,

Tony Blair would most certainly know...

'neath his thousand tooth grin and a soft double chin

something sinister I feel lies below!

Now Botox injection's another

accessory for wannabe stars,...

upper lips like balloons they will kiss like baboons,

swollen faces to hide surgeon's scars!

Hairstyling's the height of insanity...

rainbow colours, Mohican's, the lot!

For the scissors I send when those spikes stand on end

Stick the gel right up their you-know-what!

Skin piercing's the currently must have...

through lips or both ears even tongue,

I blush, don't you know, they pierce parts down below

sex enhancement I'll leave to the young!

Who cares for bell bottoms or drain-pipes?

Low trousers that show off one's bottom...

I don't think its class to show off one's arse

a cleavage that's wholly unwholesome!

Now that we're plumbing the derriere,

does a thong make you itch or feel merrier?

There's so little to view and it cuts one in two,

would you wear one to go to a premiere?

Oh my! I've forgotten the boobies!

Too big or too small that's the issue...

men seldom will quibble with upturning nipples,

with C-cup and quite real we won't argue!

So, no, I'm no follower of fashion,

let it all just hang out is my motto...

I hanker to be my pure natural me

mid-age spread I don't dread cos I'm blotto!

09.01. 2014

THE PAIN OF SEPARATION

Deep in your solar plexus a full-knuckled punch

driven hard to the midriff leaving no visible bruise

no sign of physical hurt.

No, damage is entirely cerebral,worst in early morning,

last thing at night..and through the day it comes...

repeating and repeating.

So you say to yourself, 'This too will pass,

time will heal!'

Abysmal clichés mean so little,

for a distant glimpse,

a framed photograph,

a voice in your ear,

a familiar perfume...

and she's there once again.

In your brain, in your mind,

in your soul....forever!

28.08.2012

INTO THE VOID

Leap before you look, my friend,
cast caution to the wind.
It's no time to procrastinate
or an action to rescind.

Might as well take the plunge, my friend,
fight shy of second thoughts.
Rewards may not be up to much
or in dollars with many noughts!

You've gone too far to pause, my friend,
a u-turn just won't do.
Whatever lies ahead may be
disastrous, that's quite true...

But think of something great, my friend,
success or goal achieved...
Your launch into the void could be
a result to be believed!

So clasp blind fate in both your hands,
eyes tightly closed, then jump...
you may just land upon both feet
or on your big fat rump!

17.10. 2012

THE ROOM OF NOT KNOWING

At first so bare a vacuum where

one pays no fare

rest in no chair recite a prayer

yet go nowhere

without a care no thoughts to spare

one needn't dare

breathe outside air not in this lair

first form a pair

content to share an upward stair

then tempers flare

a baleful stare

plus angry glare, he's never there

she's unaware

then errs somewhere

makes things all square

the vows they swear

no exit there..it's just not fair!

01.05.2013

HARROW ON THE HILL

Lonesome church atop the hill,

spire thrusting heavenward,

visible full three sixty.

Quiet graveyard, mottled stones inscribed

with ancient history.

Lives lived within its reach,

Byron romanticising in leafy glade...

Windsor Castle distant westwards,

far from modern life's cacophony.

Young straw-boatered gentlemen

stroll cobbled streets, coat-tails wafting

in gentle hilltop breezes.

Chapels echo, organ and choir,

tiny teahouses, clotted cream.

A journey to Harrow's past

very much alive today.

09.05.2013

PATHWAY

Can't feel my legs or anything much,

stomach like a balloon.

Tubes coming out of every place,

loved ones hovering murmuring behind their hands.

They think I don't know, but I do...I've had my time,

more than most...ninety-two summers plus.

So where's the problem...why the fuss?

Can't I be left alone to go peacefully?

Don't need these doctors, nurses with needles.

All I really need is one prick to bring it, no, I mean me

to a quick and easy end.

But no matter how my eyes entreat,

can't talk, you see, can't even scribble a message

with these quivering fingers!

They just want to keep me going...

but that's what I really want! To actually go, dammit!

Oh hell! Here they come again..I'll speak to you later,

when we meet..on the other side!

13.03.2013

MIRROR MIRROR

Two reflecting surfaces.

One before, one behind,

portray infinity.

Images become smaller, curve upwards.

Large face,

large rear.

in the distance...

Insignificant you!

Turn...

try accommodate

both left and right,

as others see you.

Peripheral vision

causing ocular strain,

for that is all we are...

peripheral.

MJD 12.06.2013

OPENING

Rampant fire breaks out.

Sparks were there always. Flames spread.

Onlookers pour insufficient to quench,

merely to appease, not extinguish.

One stands alone, encased in courage,

resists, anticipates,

creates safe periphery.

Deflects torment of those who understand little,

do not wish to comprehend

the inferno that will surely soon engulf them

already lapping at their feet...

Whence salvation?

Wisdom to recognise the obvious?

A Universal opening of minds?

Powers finally to deny

the spread of an Abomination.

14.08.2013

JUNK

I really hate to throw away

things I tend to treasure.

To gaze at ever-increasing piles

of bric-a-brac gives me pleasure.

But space has now become quite scarce,

the problem is you see,

I can't see out my windows 'cos

junk grows inordinately.

So how to ration my collection

of records, tapes and books?

A touch of arson might be on,

but insurers would give me looks!

I'll get in touch with e-bay,

hope someone will come round...

but I know just what will happen...

he'll sell me SURROUND SOUN D!

22.01.15

I WISH

I wish that all round things were square,

I wish I wasn't here but there.

I'd like to have been a movie star

but I'd have hated to have got that far.

I won't eat eggs but love a nog, my sprint looks something like a jog.

When overweight I refuse to diet..something new? I just won't try it!

I cannot think of something worse

than being accused of being perverse.

You see I like things in reverse. So when I'm happy I feel terse.

If things do seem to be going well,

I'm sure they're going straight to hell!

I hate marriage but shun divorce,

and sex needs to be a consensual force.

In the end I press restart...

I think with gut and not with heart...

and as for looks you'll see right through me...

my right arm I'd give to be George Clooney!

07.01.2015

ODE TO OSAMA

A worn sandal floating

on the ocean denoting to all of his following

'specially some who were boating

but not many churchgoing that old man remoting

while his videos were showing

blood and brain overflowing

to American gloating for nine/eleven was owing

a debt so revolting

Archbishop not coping with violence foregoing

his unease he was posting

but Prez Obama was glowing

at his men's thoroughgoing even if somewhat harrowing

with three shots they'd been mowing

eye for eye they were crowing

tooth for tooth sugar coating a ten year chapter was closing

never again touch a Boeing!

Hey! the bearded Sheikh's coasting to eternal sea-going!

11.05. 2011

MY BEST FRIEND

It wasn't fair, just twenty one,
without a care, a favourite son,
who lived each day and laughed a lot,
the things he'd say, as like as not
would crease me up and he'd just smile...
His youthful cup, quart- full meanwhile...
so suddenly, who knew from where
a scourge appeared, so hard to bear,
his life to take, our duet ended...
my heart did break, his soul ascended.

Eleven summers separated us,
same sense of fun motivated us.

Our kindred spirits, close as twins,
his life so short, devoid of sins..

Music we made, mad escapades...
still now I pine these four decades.

A boy I loved like not one other,
My Best Friend, Walt, my late kid brother.

In Loving Memory of Walter Alan Davidson who passed away 26th February 1973

RIP

05.06.2013

OFF AND ON

A marriage may be off then it's on.

An affair may be bliss then it's gone.

And ideas may be wise then to no-one's surprise

torn to shreds by all folks not just one.

A toupee may be feeling secure,

till the wind from the North strong and pure,

whips the hairpiece away when you hoped it would stay...

stronger superglue must be the cure!

You're driving along with your beau,

the satnav tells you just where to go.

Then an electronic voice gives you minimum choice

'Take the left or the right high or low!'

I was asked to write rhyme on or off,

but my chest has this too violent cough,

so I can't be a muse, that's my only excuse,

and my fever has me feeling real rough!

03.04.2014

IT'S NOT ENOUGH

It's not enough to win the race,

you must leave them all behind.

Does not suffice to be triumphant,

you need to be unkind.

Grind opponents into dust,

their discomfort you should savour.

Watch their faces twist in shame,

their dismay your sweetest flavour.

It's not so much to be the victor,

how others lose, that's fun...

don't ever think of giving mercy,

generosity you must shun.

No matter how they plead and cry,

with tears and snot they wail...

it's not enough to be on top,

your very best friend must fail!

in a rotten mood 01.05. 2012

HOW TO COMPLAIN

If there's something to gain,
and it causes no pain,
if it keeps you quite sane,
go ahead and complain!

You've got nothing to lose,
if aggression you choose...
but lay off of the booze...
keep awake, just don't snooze!

Grit your teeth and keep cool,
let them know you're no fool...
that's a negotiating tool
they don't teach in no school!

Write dozens of letters
to your elders or betters,
to creditors or debtors,
but avoid the go-getters!

When you know they are wrong,
they'll try to string you along...
in Persistence be strong,
just carry on till the gong!

Wear them down with a smile,
use cunning and guile.
Moan and groan that's the style...
pressure on you must pile!

So my advice is quite plain,
I'll say it again and again...
here's my age old refrain,
just learn how to Complain!

28.08.2014

THE JURY

I watch them enter single file.

Peruse their faces all the while.

Hoping for a ghostly smile.

Study each pale drawn profile.

My senses now so tense, fragile.

Foreman's eyes so full of guile.

Woman number four's hairstyle.

Black man number five's hostile.

Prosecutor volatile.

Have my prayers become futile?

Will I walk the deadly mile?

Did I them all so badly rile?

Do they believe I did defile

an innocent and harmless child?

Will they name me a paedophile?

16. 01. 2013

LITTLE BOY

Little boy, eyes aglow,

lost in your nether world.

A flickering screen,

where Granma's gobbled whole,

bearded chin and all,

by fungating, all-embracing, Protozoa...

Hairy multi-legged termites

smoothly slice the facial skin

of overzealous biological adventurers.

Virulent arachnids multipotently begetting,

swiftly swarming, silk-cocooning,

helpless next door neighbours!

Surely now you've had your fill?

It's late, way past your bedtime...

I'll confiscate your remote control

in just three seconds...

3...2...1

Sweet Dreams!!!

STAIN

Innocents massacred

Buildings destroyed. Artwork desecrated.

Statues demolished.

'Infidels' beheaded.

History rewritten.

Morality forgotten.

A permanent stain on the religion

they profess to uphold.

Can they be stopped?

Can a stain be removed?

Not easily, for they believe,

and non-believers must submit or die!

A veritable stain on humanity!

The Religion of Peace?

14.07.2014

THE HIPPOCRATIC OATH

You're capped and gowned

after six years of hell,

trying hard to diminish that cadaverish smell.

The ward-rounds, post-mortems, surgical errors,

Anatomy, Pathology, causing insomniac terrors!

You swear to uphold an oath that was written,

fifteen centuries before our Earth was Aids-smitten.

Your patients' well being must be central to treatment,

no finance considered before each appointment.

Dilemmas abound, when you give a prescription...

never fear ...GMC seldom brings a conviction!

Remember no-one will praise ya...

if you promote euthanasia!

So on your way, Medic students... find your way to prosperity,

as you swear to prolong

all your patient's longevity!!!

24.01.2000

THE ART OF LOSING

It's OK, you say, doesn't matter that much,

it's only a game, you're not losing your touch.

You gave of your best, or if not pretty close,

maybe he was too good, or your mind's comatose.

The fact that you're older doesn't give you excuse,

though when you thrash someone younger always gives you a boost!

You get to the end of a tough five-set match score is two all, breath hard to catch...

sweat's flooding your eyes, shirt's dripping wet,

still you're feeling so good, think you're home dry and yet...

for sure now you've got him, only two points to win...

then that brain arm connection leaves your reflexes thin.

You almost feel sorry for the guy cross the court,

till he raises his arms, he's won, you're distraught!

Look close at a winner, try to see in his eyes...

what it is in his psyche, where tenacity lies.

Defeat's not an option, he'll fight till the end, no matter what you do, he simply won't bend.

And that's how it's done, right... I'll know for next time. Think Margaret Thatcher! Let's
have you, Argentine!

17.07.2005

Occasion of Maccabi Semifinal, Israel

SUNMANIA

Bright blazing orb that fills the skies

has downside we don't realise.

Blistered lips just won't heal, flakes of skin itch then peel.

Searing pain hot water brings...tenderest touch like hornet stings!

Ghost-like pallor... creamed prevention, parasols sprouting, blessed protection!

Wobbly bits are proudly bared, tattoos and piercings shamelessly shared.

Can't be worth the looks of envy of those avoiding sun-tan frenzy.

And yet the hordes throng every year, body parts exposed in scanty wear.

Fry themselves to lobster hue so home-bound friends squeal "look at you!"

It's just as well our British Isles get solar rays like rare missiles!

We're far more used to dark grey cloud. and so each year fortnight's allowed

to pack bikinis, sun tan lotion...

sardine-like head straight for the ocean.

Turn our bodies reddish brown

drink too much beer and then fall down!

When skint and sober, just smile and say...

now that's a real good holiday!

15.4.15

THE CATCH

Aquiline, threatening,

white war-paint guards pale countenance.

Snowy flannels flapping, he lopes in express-like,

scarlet-stitched sphere fires from fist.

Receiver, armed merely with slender willow,

youthful eye-muscle reflex barely able to respond.

Feeble foot forward, studded boots nailed to earthen pitch...

contact yet puny stroke sends spinning orb in dizzy arc...

Faster than camera-lens can catch,

a body springs, arm stretched, impossibly.

Open hand meets flying object!

Resounding smack...ball rebounds in mid-air.

Trunk twisting, head and torso seemingly separated.

Fingers close round scarlet leather. Pelvis bouncing on luscious green turf.

Triumphant trophy held aloft. Fatal finger lethally points upward.

England's first wicket falls!

(Jonty Rhodes catch off bowling of Allan Donald)

STILL COMPETITIVE
(after all these years)

I wasn't always a winner, sometimes I nearly lost,

but that was when I was still young needing victory at all costs.

I jumped, ran and played so hard,

to come first was my goal...

score a try or win a match

nectar for innermost soul!

'Twas not enough just to beat the rest,

must humiliate them all,

grind their ego's into dust!

Alas! Pride comes before a Fall!

So sadly now the years run by,

muscles become quite crummy...

still Thursdays at the old folks home

I beat pants off them at Rummy!

Remains my very deepest desire,

dismembering opponents, any age...

so rheumy-eyed, double-chinned I go,

resisting life turning another page!

22.04.15

THE ATTIC

Musty, dusty, dimly lit.

Rider-less rocking horse missing a stirrup.

Motes rise as footfalls transgress

treasure trove of discarded yesterdays.

Floorboards creak, woven webs traverse vast spaces.

Pictureless frames gathering dirt

that once displayed such splendours.

A scuttling noise, a rodent surely, protesting an invasion of its lair.

Decaying atmosphere of unwantedness,

peruses nether regions .

Ancient wardrobe boasts tarnished mirror.

I see myself as I am now.

Not young as in shelved mouldy albums.

But at age of reflection, wizened, drawn.

Visiting my attic,

I am perusing my very own grave.

31.08.2011

LET THERE BE LIGHT

That's what the Lord said, in the beginning.

And Lo! There was Light! And He saw that it was Good.

Then His Creatures came. Made noises of communication.

Like UG! FSSS! BRUB!

Romance was a Wooden Club Millenia passed.

Men walked upright, conversed, wrote, sang, sometimes even in rhyme.

Tongues in glorious mellow tones, flirtatious French, guttural German,

Ardent Italian, seductive Spanish, indecipherable Danish,

and evergreen English, Shakespeare's voice...

Romance was Midsummer Night Dreaming.

Then the Lord said... Let there be Microsoft! And Bill Gates came to pass.

Men Googled, Yahoo'd, became Browsers, developed Interface.

Double-clicked Dotcoms, forward-slashed Enron...

became subservient to Servers enmeshed in World-wide Web!

Resided in Chat-rooms, spent hours Surfing, Browsing, Pasting, Copying.

A Mouse which Megabytes, occasional break to Download.

Email users, Online Dating, Porno and Paedo abusers...

Files corrupted by Trojan Viruses...

Romance Via Cyberspace!

(Come back Byron,...all is forgiven!)

30.01.2001

ON BEING A FATHER OF THE BRIDE-TO-BE

As father of the bride to be,

I haven't slept a wink.....

they say each moment must be savoured or

they'll pass by in a blink!

I've tried some drugs that didn't work,

perhaps next I'll try a drink,

or failing that get desperate

and phone the nearest shrink!

They say you cannot take it with you,

so what the hell , relax......

just spend your loot on daughter fair,

more fun than paying Tax!

And as the Wedding Day draws near,

just take a deep, deep breath.......

put on your suit and shiny shoes

and dance yourself to death!

15.07.2011

FRATERNITY

Reality dawns so sudden though,

may always have been there to see

what lay beneath external warmth,

sheer blood-panged jealousy.

Two lifetimes lived alongside,

futures intertwined.

Families so closely linked,

who knew what lurked behind.

If one had looked, had probed too deep,

through rosy years that passed,

even then, maybe, this malignant swell

might not have grown so fast.

But now as vicious tide sweeps in,

ancient anger tars the sands...

no return to submerged depths,

this is how forever stands.

12.05.2003

O DAUGHTER MY DAUGHTER

The room is bare, your presence gone,

a cloud obscures our sun...

Carpet lies undressed, carelessly flung

emblems of your being here once.

Clothing, boots , trainers, CD covers

reminiscent by their absence.

Symbolically adorned walls now

sad displays of sellotape scars.

Wardrobes still retain within

flecks of your oh so short sojourn.

Deep at night reverberating hum

of bass guitar's repeated phrases...

melodies of your soul,

ear pressed to your door I hear them still.

Melancholy I am not, witnessing your growth,

your flight to world of hope

and fulfilment.

2006

I'M ALONE

I'm on my own.

Friends I thought once were, now shrink away.

Even become my foes.

I'm surrounded, hearing their growling malevolence.

Taking nips from my nether regions.

I strike out with vigour. Their yelping just crescendoes.

I feel, no, I know I am superior.

Could that be reason for their hatred?

All I ever desired is so simple. To be left to live in peace.

Yet they hate me.

I am sure I have been here forever.

It is they who intrude.

I have few doubts however slim.

I make sounds of compromise. To no avail.

They grow stronger. So I need to grow more cunning.

My back is to a wall of blue.

Where will it end?

Only God knows.

29.03..2012

STIFF UPPER LIP

Biting lower lip to mince,

swallowing hard,

stifling sobs.

Wiping nose,

adjusting shades

to hide salt tears.

With each hug

and tight embrace,

diaphragm heaves.

Many hours and days you've known

what's just around the bend,

yet when that final moment comes

all bets are off...

unashamedly you cry,

but...

how many times can you say good bye?

25.07.2012

SEMITIC SIAMESE

Born in blood, confusion.

Biblical brothers with land to share.

Inseparably fused face to face.

One heart of gold, city atop ochre shaded hills.

World's wise men gathered...Flushing Meadow, Nineteen forty seven.

Cast votes one chilled November eve, hailed infants arrival side by side.

Partition! Surgical Solution!

Separate the indivisible... though joined head to toe!

Naivete to span generations to come.

Six decades of death have passed.

Two babes enmeshed in strife eternal.

One transfused with life and vigour,

the other immersed in suicidal loathing.

Still wise men pontificate

on twins long-term survival.

Nature's Law in time applies.

Weaker will succumb to strong!

15.09.2002

MILK AND HONEY

Mother Hen gathering in her Diasporic chicks.

Gifted, multi-tongued, a spectral people,

laying claim to baked unleavened land.

Rocks and dust, transformed to greening,

sparing droplets greedily sucked

through infinitely pierced serpents

'neath shimmering lakes of plastic.

Metal tentacles thrust cloudwards,

horizons ruptured with relentless vigour,

astride thorny spurs projecting

from previous untilled undergrowth.

Yelping with constant pain, yet these she flattens

with unassailable certainty.

This land is ours. Mine. For I am one of them.

Not only now...

but since ever I can recall.

And forever.

15.04.2001

IN RECLINE

Blinding sun shining, filtered through Perspex.

Cloven air to breathe...

tiny bee-sting in the hollow

of my bared elbow.

Surrounded by masked concern,

nailless rubber hands wave above me,

wielding sparkling silver scythes.

White-robed ghosts

waft nearer,

humming harmoniously,

accompanying my sacro-iliac stretching.

Ears sponge-sheltered,

Puccini, my choice.,

Warmth enveloping limbs then torso,

neck and chin.

Far beyond my vulnerable self

I open wide...

15.11.2001

FOG

Invisible birdsong filters through barren boughs.

From my window a silver-shrouded forest silently surveys

its dampened moss-brown mattress.

Babbling voices from the past pierce my stillness.

Familiar countenances blurring in swirling mist

of this lonely gloomy room.

Pictures framed of long-lost loved ones encircle my horizon.

Well-intentioned intrusions shatter the cell of my solitude.

I partly recognise them...I do not welcome them.

Platters thrust before me, gelatinous mash, coloured capsules to be swallowed.

Smell of winter emanates from my body. Carers come, leave me unwashed.

Men conversing, beloved sons distantly whispering.

Can this be how it all ends?

No-one knows or understands to what strange place I have retreated.

Just a vessel to be fed, sedated, till nature takes its merciful course.

Could I fly, spirited, disembodied, beyond these leaded windows,

through misty gardens to undemanding forest?

To rest forever blanketed beneath its cloud-covered embrace?

Remembering Sadie 15.01.2004

TXT RYM

2 sherin code

2 txt in case

1 cud erode

Th othr's bas

I no jst hw

2 strt yr ca

Yr grshft now

Wl strtch qte fa

It wl respond

2 bt 1 tch

So dn't abscnd

Lv u 2 mch

Yr clphn vlntin

2001.

THE CHAIR BENEATH THE TREE

A spreading oak, cascading acorns,

stands alone beyond expansive lawn's reach.

Blocking sunlight, creating its own halo.

He used to sit there, pipe alight, eyes rheumy from the smoke.

Gnarled fists clasped as if entreating.

A straw hat shielding him

from daylight already shaded.

Gazing back at us, cavorting,

with that sunken grin.

An ageing man, contented

with his life's work.

The chair still sits beneath the oak tree,

we cannot consider its removal.

Wooden slats mouldy, metal rusting.

But momentarily, just close our eyes and....

he is there once more.

04.07. 2012

FOOTWEAR FAILURE

Apologies to Rogers and Hammerstein 'Carousel' and Liverpool FC

When you walk with new shoes do your toes cramp and cry?

You falter then you stumble and you fall...

Fancy styles you may choose, many pairs you may try,

you can bet what you get are too small!

Walk on through the pain...they'll never take them back again

'cause the sweat and the blood are your own!

Walk on, stagger on, hope they'll stretch or you're done

and the blisters may get to the bone...

You'll always limp alone!

Walk home, go straight in, throw those shoes in the bin,

sod the cost and please just don't moan...

fluffy slippers for you alone!

When you're home, on the phone, bathe your feet with a groan...

tacky trainers... no more shoes from now on!

Then you'll never walk alone!

MJD 30.04. 2014

MALIGNANCY

A cell divides irregularly.

A misfit multiplies, spreads,

infecting its fellows.

Pacific code warped into aggressive mode,

permeating flatulent host.

Silently.

Minuscule attacks from within protected lairs.

Always amongst the innocent,

Gulliverian victim lashes out,

harshly, hastily.

Mostly ineffectual.

Metastases abound, a creeping hypnotic seeding,

followed by Grand Mal germination.

Flailing response from those

who rain humanitarian manna.

To no avail.

All live on TV.

04.10.2001

UNREQUITED

Yearning. Painstakingly disguised

lest merest murmur escape, slimed by common mouths.

(I'm sure she doesn't know)

Hours, years fly by.

Tender hopes flutter beneath my heaving breastbone.

(I think I want her to know)

Hesitant approaches come to nought.

Common-sense decrees now surely passion's euthanasia.

(I pray she'll never know)

Yet...occasional corneal contact

windowing carnality yields fresh wild imaginings.

(Could she possibly know)

"Enough!" cries cruel logic.

"Retreat! Dignity!"

I embrace forlorn senility.

(I'm sure she never knew)

05.06.1997

VAITING AND VAITING

Outside a Chinese restaurant the Rabbi looked inside,

he rubbed his eyes in disbelief and thru his beard he sighed...

"Dat surely isn't Moishe Pipick, my congregant so devout....

vots goin' to eat dat goyishe traif, vot should I do, call out?"

The Rabbi then decided to wait and keeping shtum

watched his Moishe order pork and lots of shrimp dim sum!

He waited several minutes more, observing Moishe eat,

mega mouthfuls verkakte ribs, enjoying it a treat!

Eventually he could wait no more,

yelled through the door "OY VAY!

Moishe Pipick, you schlemiel, you can't transgress dis way!

How can you gobble all dis traif, and lick your lips to boot?

Then come and pray in Shul

in your smart shiny Shabbas suit?"

"Hold on a minute," Moishe said,

"you saw me come in here?"

"You saw me sit down at this bench and order all this fare?"

The Rabbi now was quite confused,

and nodded, "Yes, for sure."

"You saw the waiter bring this food,

all fried and sizzling pure?"

"And then you saw me eat it all, leaving not one crumb?"

The Rabbis said "Mit my own eyes,

you think I'm kinda dumb?"

"Well OK then" cool Moishe grinned,

"why mount this Inquisition?

My entire meal was eaten under Rabbinical Supervision!"

12.06.2012

(from a joke sent to me by Janice of WIZO PE South Africa)

PAVLOVA PANIC

EIGHTEEN FOR LUNCH WERE INVITED,
FRIENDS, NEIGHBOURS, SOME EASY, SOME POSH.
SUNDAY DAWNED BRIGHTLY, FOR ENGLAND...
I SET OFF EARLY FOR MY GAME OF SQUASH.
GOT HOME, HAVING BEEN SOUNDLY BEATEN,
BY MUCH YOUNGER MAN, MUST BE SAID,
I HEARD SCREAMING FROM 'HER INDOORS' KITCHEN,
FOUR-LETTER WORDS TURNED MY FACE RED!
MADAME'S PIECE DE RESISTANCE, PAVLOVA, A MASSIVE MERINGUE
WORK OF ART,
SHE WAS SURE HAD BEEN STEALTHILY INVADED
BY HUGE SPIDER, NEARLY STOPPING HER HEART!
"KEEP CALM" SAID I, ALWAYS THE BRAVE ONE.
"YOU SURE YOU SAW IT FOR CERTAIN?"
'I'M NOT BLIND, YES! I SAW IT, WITH HAIRS ON...
BEASTLY THING RAN STRAIGHT DOWN OFF THE CURTAIN!'
"FIRST THING TO BE DONE IS TO FIND IT," I SAID, HELD UP A
BARBECUE LANCE.
"BY CREATING EMERGENCY EXIT WE'LL PROD AND OUT IT WILL
PRANCE!"
I STABBED THE MERINGUE WITH ABANDON,
PERFORATING ITS WHITENESS ALL OVER,
BUT ALAS! THE ARACHNID STAYED HIDDEN,
PROBLY GORGING ON WIFE'S SWEET PAVLOVA!
HAVING TURNED DESSERT INTO GRUYERE,
I CEASED MY ASSAULT THERE AND THEN.
"NO SPIDER IN THERE" I ASSERTED,
"LET'S SIT DOWN AND COUNT UP TO TEN!"
'THERE'S TIME FOR MAKING ANOTHER.
.. OUR GUESTS WON'T BE HERE FOR A MINUTE.'
WIFE LIFTED INFECTED CONFECTION...
'ONLY ONE THING TO DO, THAT'S TO BIN IT!'
"NO, DON'T, THAT'S INCREDIBLY WASTEFUL"
I POINTED TO SUMMER FRUIT FILLING.
"WHY NOT FILL IT AND COME OUT ALL TRUTHFUL,
TELL OUR GUESTS WHAT IT IS THEY'LL BE SWILLING!"
"SUGGEST DESSERT GAME, CALL IT 'CHICKEN'.
..WHOEVER GETS SLICE WITH THE SPIDER...
WINS FIRST PRIZE... A DELISH FINGERLICKIN'
SECOND PIECE WITH NO SPIDER INSIDER!"
IN THE END MY SUGGESTION WAS VETOED,

NO SENSE MIXING PROTEIN WITH SWEET,
THE WIFE, CULINARY WIZARD, PROCEEDED,
TO BAKE ANOTHER, NOT ADMITTING DEFEAT.
LUNCH CAME AND WENT WELL, SMOOTH AS TOFFEE,
MERINGUE NUMBER TWO WAS A HIT!
THEN TIME CAME FOR CHEESE AND FOR COFFEE,
THE CUE FOR ME DOING MY BIT!
I POURED THE GUESTS EACH A LARGE ONE,
DISPLAYING MY SKILL WITH THE BREW...
TILL THE LAST, LADY DOTTY FFYFE –HAMILTON
IN WHOSE CUP FLOATED SPIDER, WELL- STEWED!
DOWAGER PASSED CLEAN OUT AT TABLE,
AMPLY CUSHIONED BY A FORTY-SIX CHEST...
TABLE TOP WAS REGRETTABLY UNSTABLE,
TOTAL CONTENTS CAME OFF SECOND BEST!
"MY COFFEE SET, MY CHEESE DISH!" YELLED WIFE.
"MY WIFE !" SHOUTED DOTTY'S POOR SPOUSE.
"MY BRAND NEW SILK BLOUSE" BLUBBERED DOROTHY,
I QUIETLY CREPT OUT OF THE HOUSE!
DEAR HOSTESS, THIS NIGHTMARISH LESSON.
.. TO STOP HONOURED GUESTS ALL FROM BITCHIN',
WHEN TARANTULA'S AROUND, IF IT'S NOT QUICKLY FOUND,
KEEP HUSBAND RIGHT OUT OF THE KITCHEN!!!!

10.05.2001

WIND

Where does it come from, where does it go?

This current of air, the wind that doth blow?

It shivers the leaves, hunchbacks the trees,

chief Flight Assistant to swarmed bumble bees.

In ancient times did swell the sails

of galleons in pursuit of whales.

Now hillsides harness-ed with vanes

windmill towers to power Mains.

Malevolent breeze, the hurricane

frequents Costa Americaine,

whilst desert sand in sculptures form

dunes remoulded by the storm.

But illest wind, though gusts be small...

that which emanates from us all!

From 'Odd Bedfellows' 1998

FRANCIS ALBERT : 15ᵀᴴ MAY, 1998

The day Sinatra died...

What did I Do? I cried.

How Little We Know

What got Under his Skin

We Came and Flew with him,

Began his Beguine!

Softly as he Left Us In The Wee Small Hours Of The Morning

He'll Never Smile Again or holler Ring-a- Ding Ding!

Luck was his Lady

Night and Day

Love and Marriage He did them His Way

He loved to go Travelling Chicago New York or Rome

He made it There, He made it Everywhere

Now at last He's Home

What did I do, the day Ol' Blue Eyes died?

Had One For My Baby, sat still, tuned in

and cried...

Odd Bedfellows 1998

EMPTYNESS

The film is over, popcorn eaten,

ushers with their torches gone...

Movie-goers homeward streaming,

inside cinema dark, forlorn.

DEATH

Death, the only certainty in Life

apart from Pain.

One inevitably leading to the other.

Some, more fortune-struck, escape

with suddenness, by catastrophic bleeding,

whilst others shrink through months and years,

showing merely bones and skin.

Heartfelt pleas to end it all

'Kill me, let me die in peace.'

Odd Bedfellows 1998.

Lightning Source UK Ltd.
Milton Keynes UK
UKOW04f1050170216

268542UK00002B/90/P